# John Hawkes
# and the Craft of Conflict

# John Hawkes and the Craft of Conflict

By John Kuehl

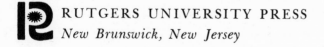
RUTGERS UNIVERSITY PRESS
*New Brunswick, New Jersey*

The author and publisher are grateful for permission to quote from the following books. The specific references are documented in the notes.

*Space, Time and Structure in the Modern Novel,* by Sharon Spencer, copyright © by New York University.

*Nausea,* by Jean-Paul Sartre, translated by Lloyd Alexander, copyright © 1964 by New Directions Publishing Corporation. All rights reserved.

*From Ritual to Romance,* by Jessie L. Weston, copyright © Cambridge University Press.

*The Greek Myths,* by Robert Graves, by permission of the author and A. P. Watt & Son.

*The American Novel and Its Traditions,* by Richard Chase, copyright © by Doubleday & Company, Inc.

*A Handbook to Literature,* by C. Hugh Holman, based on the original by William Flint Thrall and Addison Hibbard, copyright © 1972 by the Bobbs-Merrill Company, Inc.

*Civilization and Its Discontents,* by Sigmund Freud, copyright © by W. W. Norton & Company, Inc.

*Library of Congress Cataloging in Publication Data*

Kuehl, John Richard, 1928–
    John Hawkes and the craft of conflict.

    Bibliography: p.
    1.  Hawkes, John, 1925–   —Criticism and
interpretation.   I.   Title.
PS3558.A82Z75        813'.5'4        74-34088

ISBN 0-8135-0802-9

For Little Kwell

## SPECIAL THANKS TO

John Hawkes, for his generous cooperation;
Curt Greer, for supplying copies of Mr. Hawkes's poems;
The Arts and Science Research Fund of New York University for financial assistance;
L. F., and E. B. for their valuable criticisms;
L. V. K. for her constant encouragement and support;
My wife, Linda Kandel Kuehl, for much besides help with the revisions.

# Contents

# Preface

There has been a marked discrepancy between the academic and the general reception of John Hawkes's novels. Eminent literary critics such as Albert J. Guerard, Leslie A. Fiedler, Robert Scholes, and Tony Tanner have praised his art, yet Hawkes commands only a small following, many of whom are college teachers and students. Popular reviewers and their audience, failing to comprehend how his work operates, also fail to understand what it expresses.

Those who expect formal and conceptual materials associated with traditional realism are perplexed, for Hawkes mocks these as anachronistic. Substituting "vision" for "novel" and "reality" for "realism," he would support Robbe-Grillet's contention that verisimilitude is no longer the issue. Old familiar fictional elements—plot, character, setting, and theme—seem banal to an anti-realist who rightly considers himself unique. But rather than abandoning such elements altogether, Hawkes has used them increasingly for parodic purposes as his work moves from grim surrealism to comic realism. The resulting manipulation of complicated techniques and attitudes makes him one of the most difficult American novelists since William Faulkner.

The negative reaction to his work may be explained in part by the very qualities that, in other quarters, have earned him serious critical acclaim. The pleasures derived from Hawkes's prose are the pleasures derived from poetry. If the reader does not appreciate rhetorical, tonal, and structural complexity, as well as paradox, he will not respond. Nor will he respond if he demands logic and solace, because this fiction communicates objectively and uncompromisingly the nightmarish aspects of irrational twentieth-century experience.

The rewards that come from reading John Hawkes are great, for he is probably the most gifted living exponent of grotesque literary art. To obtain them, one must value the formal beauty of energized language, imaginative settings, elaborate structures, bizarre characters, and ironic narrative foci. And one must confront the conceptual ugliness of human depravity. In short, enjoying Hawkes's work depends on aesthetic sensitivity and philosophical detachment.

Two books have been written about him. One, Frederick Busch's *Hawkes: A Guide to His Fiction,* clarifies what happens in the novels. The other, Donald Greiner's *Comic Terror,* analyzes the nature of their humor. Though both books—and some articles—recognize and occasionally explore the connection between form and content in his art, no previous study has been exclusively devoted to this subject.

Hawkes's novels constitute worlds more separate and distinct from each other than those of any contemporary American author except, perhaps, Vladimir Nabokov. Certain formal and conceptual patterns nevertheless run through them all, giving his canon its own special stamp.

The formal patterns, which involve landscapes and settings, myths and rituals, structure, characterization, and narrative focus, convey several conceptual patterns. The most important is the tension between Eros (love/life) and Thanatos (death).

This tension first appears in *The Lime Twig* (1961). Before then, Hawkes's work was exclusively death-oriented, but afterwards Eros exists alongside Thanatos in his view of human and external nature.

The techniques used prior to 1961 suit a tensionless universe where Thanatos reigns supreme, and those used later reflect the conflict produced by the advent of Eros. Decentralized form gives way to dramatic form: static landscapes become dynamic, negative myths and rituals ambivalent, flat characters round, circular structures linear, and mixed narrative voices one narrative voice. Hawkes's techniques come to project the paradox of a writer considered darkly pessimistic by many but comically optimistic by himself, for they show Eros and Thanatos sharing ultimate victory.

Under the assumption that form and content are inseparable in major art, this book treats the relationship between Hawkes's central theme and his craft, and simultaneously traces the evolution of both. Chapter 1 focuses on landscapes and settings, 2 on myths and rituals, 3 on structure, 4 on characterization, and 5 on narrative focus. Chapter 6 demonstrates how such formal devices function in a single novel, *The Blood Oranges,* to dramatize the Life-

Force versus Death-Force opposition introduced and developed earlier. The last section, "Interview," records some of the author's own comments on his work.

New directions has published all six Hawkes novels: *The Cannibal* (1949), *The Beetle Leg* (1951), *The Lime Twig* (1961), *Second Skin* (1964), *The Blood Oranges* (1971), *Death, Sleep & the Traveler* (1974). In 1966 New Directions made available *The Innocent Party: Four Short Plays by John Hawkes* (*The Innocent Party, The Wax Museum, The Undertaker, The Questions*) and in 1969, *Lunar Landscapes: Stories & Short Novels 1950–1963* ("The Traveler," 1962; "The Grandmother," 1961; "A Little Bit of the Old Slap and Tickle," 1962; "Death of an Airman," 1950; "A Song Outside," 1962; "The Nearest Cemetery," 1963; *Charivari*, 1950; *The Owl*, 1954; *The Goose on the Grave*, 1954). These volumes are the source of the textual quotations that follow.

John Hawkes
and the Craft of Conflict

# 1

# Landscapes of the Imagination

To Hawkes—and to Faulkner, whom he admires —history means war. Hawkes's contention, "Everything I've written comes out of nightmare, out of the nightmare of war, I think," [1] seems but slightly exaggerated, for, if *Charivari* and *The Beetle Leg* among the novels preceding *The Blood Oranges*, the four plays, and scattered poems and stories are excluded, this nightmare haunts all his landscapes. Conflicts other than the Second World War emerge: *The Cannibal* treats World War I and throughout there are numerous allusions to a martial past, its principal setting being the thousand-year-old camp site Spitzen-on-the-Dein; *The Owl*, with its warscape around Sasso Fetore, treats vague pre-/post-Renaissance struggles. World War II, however, is Hawkes's focal war; it dominates at least four novels (*The Goose on the Grave, The Cannibal, The Lime Twig, Second Skin*) and four stories ("Death of an Airman," "The Grandmother," "The Traveler," "A Little Bit of the Old Slap and Tickle").

Hawkes does not care much about military strategy or

combat, though he burlesques both through mock battles—for example, the anti-heroine Stella's march on the asylum in *The Cannibal*. Chosen to restore order there, she leads an army of savage deputized females wearing black puttees and shouldering barrel-staves against a troop of ridiculous male inmates while their Director studies his files. This onslaught ends with the women victorious over several mutilated corpses—apparently little men, actually frozen monkeys. Most military tactics and encounters are so masked, but many other wartime situations and events remain manifest. That Hawkes is drawn more toward the aftermath of war than war itself Skipper, the narrator of *Second Skin*, confirms: "The night I found Fernandez on Second Avenue was the first night after the day they stopped the war, and . . . . all my casualties . . . were only accidents that came when the wave of wrath was past."

During the unpublished B.B.C. broadcast entitled "The Landscape of the Imagination," where Hawkes said "Everything I've written comes . . . out of the nightmare of war," he called *The Cannibal*'s extraordinary metaphor describing Spitzen-on-the-Dein "as shrivelled in structure and as decomposed as an ox's tongue, black with ants" archetypical "of the world I care most about." This early novel lacks the episodic organization and sympathetic rogue-hero identified with picaresque fiction; nevertheless, its "landscape of sexless apathy" brought to mind the Spanish picaresque writers, particularly Quevedo. According to Hawkes, in *Buscón* "the decomposed, deracinated, deteriorated physical world is the setting for grotesque humour." There "all of our aspirations and our worst fears are somehow actualized." [2]

*The Cannibal* epitomizes Hawkes's warscapes. In the first chapter alone there are innumerable tokens of conflict littering a foreground where nearly every token of community has been shattered. Spitzen-on-the-Dein (*Spitzen:* summit; *Dein:* your, Rhine?) possesses no eating places or food. Bells do not ring, people do not talk "except for fragments of a sentence," and accompanying the prevailing silence are moldly smells. Wash hangs out, fires burn, cobwebs appear. Inmates, thieves, beggars, and prisoners wander about at will. Institutions and private businesses have collapsed. The theater shows "each day the same blurred picture to no audience"; the butcher shop contains only a few unsold, unsanctioned "cold strands of flesh"; and the embalmer cannot administer formaldehyde. Gone are the normal conveniences and services. Gone too are healthy animals and plants. The fields lack men and beasts to cultivate them.

In this town, where the population remains static, everybody wears gray and some sport military attire: "coats with epaulettes and brass buttons" for the women; "pasteboard Teutonic helmets" for the children, who roam "in small bands . . . their faces scratched and nails long." Formerly a *grande dame*, Stella is now a landlady; her sister, Jutta, once a novitiate, is now an adulteress. Their associates exhibit similar incongruity: the homosexual cannibal is a duke; the madman, Balamir, a prince; the assassin, Zizendorf, a leader. In his editorial capacity, the last has fingers "too blunt to punch the keys," but he seems no less qualified for this work than other characters—an alcoholic voyeur for census-taking, a nympholeptic tuba player for school-teaching. The publisher of the *Crooked Zeitung* and the officials of the asylum have vanished, and the Mayor and the Signalman have become ineffectual.

Spitzen-on-the-Dein's metropolitan counterpart, *das Grab* (the Grave) of Part II, shows how landscape alters during war. One setting, the *Sportswelt Brauhaus* (Sportsworld Tavern), is particularly vivid. Hawkes depicts it before World War 1 as "austere and licensed, patronized and rushed upon." At that time the well-lighted room had severe tables and chairs, white walls, a high ceiling. Black-jacketed waiters served food and beer to straight-backed, disciplined-looking officers and their powerful, rigid Nordic girlfriends, while a loud Bavarian trio accompanied Stella, the new singer, a sorceress with large breasts, showy hips, gold hair. From the Sportswelt Brauhaus on the hot night ten days prior to the assassination of Franz Ferdinand sounds of laughter and talk drifted towards the garden, where, along with other blossoms, German-valor-petals and cannon flowers gave off an intoxicating scent.

This pre-war setting, which Hawkes renders ironically, is self-destructive, for here Stella or Germania presides over Aryan comrades who historicize myth and mythicize history. Her Scandinavian ancestors "cloaked themselves in animal skins" and "carved valorous battles on their shields," so she becomes more and more assimilated by tradition as she sings. The daughter of the old General represents chivalric grace and breeding. Her boyfriend, Ernst, the son of the Brauhaus owner, wishes to sit "in the hall of kings," though he cannot enter military combat because one hand has been mutilated. Stella grows erotic staring at it and his dueling scars.

During World War I, the Sportswelt Brauhaus is transformed. Outside lawns are uncut, valor-petals dry, leaves dead. Inside there are overturned tables, unusable chairs, dusty planks. Girls and schnapps are gone, and children peer through windows toward chaos. "Vandals, with tunics itching on bare chests, with packs paining and eyes red," await orchestra, lights, singer, but the stage holds only "periodicals and lists of the dead." These vandals have displaced the straight-backed officers and a trollop has displaced sorceress Stella. Her appearance—sharp hips and lopsided lips, "a little more sallow, a little more old"—differs radically from Stella's on that hot pre-war evening.

In *The Cannibal* human beings experience many hardships, but the most striking impact of war is its direct physical assault upon the individual. Many, like Stella's mother, die violently, unexpectedly. Corpses are grotesque: the Merchant, dead on the first day, "was wedged standing upright, between two beams, his face knocked backwards, angry, disturbed." A cocoon still webs his mouth when he is found near the Brauhaus latrine months later. Others defy burial under even more watery circumstances. While the American overseer is being disposed of in a swamp, "bodies . . . slowly appeared one by one . . . from the mud." People may escape destruction and exposure only to be wounded or mutilated: the soldiers of Spitzen return with ears chopped off, the son of Stella "with . . . stump and steel canes."

In *The Lime Twig* the present action occurs ten years after World War II. It illustrates how lasting is the impact of such conflicts. Michael and Margaret Banks were children during that war, a struggle she does not even remember. Descending upon their boarding house, where his now deceased mother and he then lived, is William Hencher, "the purveyor of the seeds of war," who "was important to [Hawkes] in order to bring the war forward into the adult lives of Michael and Margaret." [3] This lodger had once entered a crashed bomber, grasped the wheel, and adjusted the helmet, "my bloody coronet in place at last." Determined to seize the Bankses' home, he joins the Aldington racetrack mob, all of whose members have been perverted by their wartime experiences. They ensnare Michael and Margaret as easily as limed branches ensnare birds. Michael is the perfect dupe, for drab post-war England has caused him to dream about a horse Hencher urges him to steal. This dream, promising violent sexual fulfillment also craved by Margaret, leads to their death. In a sense, then, the Bankses are as much "casualties" of the war as Hencher and his fellow mobsters.

The metaphor of World War II, which dominates Hawkes's landscapes between 1949 and 1964, resembles *The Waste Land* in its international aspects. He treats Germany (*The Cannibal*), England (*The Lime Twig*), Italy (*The Goose on the Grave*), and North America (*Second Skin*). Unlike Eliot, however, who considered World War I the final collapse of a once great civilization, Hawkes thinks of World War II as merely another instance of human aggression.

His landscapes are not altogether imaginary. Though often remote and sometimes exotic, most arise from the actual world directly apprehended. Hawkes started *The Cannibal* after reading about a real cannibal in Bremen and *The Lime Twig* after reading about legalized gambling in England. He had been to Germany before writing *The Cannibal*, Italy before *The Owl* and *The Goose on the Grave*, the American West before *The Beetle Leg*, the West Indies before *Second Skin*, but these books are as "mythical" as *Charivari* and *The Lime Twig*, which he wrote without visiting England. His geographical locations combine dream-like familiarity and unfamiliarity, so Hawkes, a non-realist too, admires Flannery O'Connor's and Nathanael West's "improbable yet fictionally true" [4] settings.

In 1964 he said that the novels had begun "with mere germs of ideas," not narrative elements or specific characters; what attracted him was "a landscape or world . . . something immediately and intensely visual—a room, a few figures, an object." Such pictures, "prompted by the initial idea and then literally seen," he compared to "the visual images that come to us just before sleep." [5] Infantile wishes and sexual anxieties abound. These and other distorted psychic materials liberated from Hawkes's unconscious suggest nightmare with its violence and grotesque humor.

He respects the surrealistic movement whose use of dream projections he shares, but he eschews simple unconscious flow or automatic writing. His shaped and controlled novels have undergone considerable revision and reconception and his vocabulary has made certain psychological and literary terms interchangeable, "unconscious" becoming "imagination," "dream" becoming "vision." Hawkes tries to actualize the imagination, to create, not record, and success depends upon how well consciousness can impose a pattern on unconscious material.

Remote, exotic, vague landscapes do more than liberate him. They provide detachment, and detachment is uniquely important to an author who feels only antipathy toward autobiographical fiction. When he exploits his own psychic life, he does so impersonally and because his psychic life reveals the general psychic life. Hawkes, who may be viewed as an instrument of Jung's "collective unconscious," consciously molds universal archetypes into works of art. Produced by interaction between consciousness and unconsciousness themselves, these works of art treat various dichotomies, such as rational against irrational, subjective reality against objective reality.

Otto Rank calls myth "a dream of the masses of the people," and in this context Hawkes's novels are mythic. But they are also historic, since history, man's conscious record, and myth, man's unconscious record, merge. History-become-myth permeates *The Cannibal* which satirizes the chauvinism associated with modern Germany. That sentimental politics may mask military ambition is made clear when an expatriate English traitor grows quixotic over Antwerp:

The Krupp gun, 42 centimeter, took them through and luckily enough, I was able to see the whole thing. It was like Hohenlohe's progress in Africa, more, you see, than just a concentration of men for their own good, more than anything like a unity of states, like the Zolleverein, rather complete success, a mass move greater than a nation, a more pure success than Prussia's in the Schleswig-Holstein affair. We fought, gained in the area of Soissons and they couldn't drive us from Saint Mihiel—glory be to the German army!

This example of history-become-myth is matched during *The Cannibal* by examples of myth-become-history. To names evoking a mythological Scandinavian past like Jutta (Jutland) and Balamir (Ymir) should be added Valhalla, where Le Comte de Gobineau argued true Aryans went. The anti-heroine Stella accepts Odin's paradise of slain heroes and would join boyfriend Ernst there. Just as her illusions stem from a private history that boasts brave Norwegian ancestors, the illusions of the nation she personifies originate with a public history that insists upon the same pure racial heritage. Numerous blackly comic references to Nordic and Teutonic appear in the book, one in the neofascist dictator Zizendorf's Indictment: "the land, the Teutonic land, gives birth to the strongest of races, the Teutonic race." These references suggest how romantic the dual processes of history-become-myth and myth-become-history are. They produce cannibalistic, self-devouring fantasies which deprive men of a real time and a real place and which destroy their humanity and their identity.

After 1964 war ceases to dominate Hawkes's work, but his landscapes continue to be imaginary though recognizable, often remote and sometimes exotic, as the four short plays published during 1966 demonstrate. One occurs at "an abandoned motel in a subtropical area of the United States"; one at "a wax museum in a small Canadian beach resort"; one at "an old-fashioned lavatory"; one at a courtroom or doctor's office or sun parlor. Such familiar nonfamiliar landscapes would seem fitting for plays preoccupied with unconscious forces.

The conflicts in these plays all have sexual connotations. *The Innocent Party* presents a young girl, "part tomboy and part Aphrodite," torn between a lesbian aunt and prudish parents. Sisters beneath the skin, *The Wax Museum*'s erotically belligerent attendant and virginally submissive fiancée exchange garments, then roles. In *The Undertaker,* a death-oriented father, who has already destroyed his wife, climaxes the damage done his son by committing suicide in front of him. In *The Questions,* a fantasy-ridden daughter, who has felt a reciprocated attraction toward her impuissant father, recalls the adulterous affair between her promiscuous mother and her father's friend.

These last two plays are psychodramas. Because *The Undertaker* treats an experience that happened when the son was twelve, though not staged until his mid-forties, it is a memory play somewhat like *The Glass Menagerie*. Similarly, landscape in *The Questions* may be "the pure space of psychic activity" (the mind of the daughter) as well as courtroom, doctor's office, or sun parlor.

Since the individual unconscious reflects the collective unconscious, infantile psychic states are paralleled by primordial mythic states. Paradise lost, one primitive setting that recurs throughout Hawkes's work, indicates that his mythic states also have a latent sexual-aggressive content. The following exchange between the lesbian aunt and the prudish parents in *The Innocent Party* almost makes this explicit:

PHOEBE: Can you imagine an ambulance in here? The long white emergency arm of medical science in the Garden of Eden . . . . Interns in white uniforms fighting their way through the orchids . . . . Janie would love that.

BEATRIX: It's not paradise. Believe me.

PHOEBE: You think it's not? Orchids, bougainvillea, acacia trees, all these doves and the swamp moss like frozen mist—lots of people would call it paradise.

BEATRIX: This place? Look around you, Phoebe. Look around you at desolation. No electricity, no water in the swimming pool, no telephone . . . .

EDWARD: She's right, Phoebe. The lines are down.

BEATRIX: Dust and weeds and rampant jungle and rotting mattresses in empty rooms. There aren't even any screens on the windows. Someone slashed all the screens on the windows. With a knife . . . .

PHOEBE: An inexpensive retreat amidst luxuriant growth, baby. What more do you want? It's beautiful.

BEATRIX: An abandoned motel on the edge of the universe. It smells of obsolescence and rank decay, it smells of the tears of uncouth strangers and the refuse of sordid pleasures. It smells of death.

Why did war, an even more extreme landscape of infantile/primordial aggression, cease to dominate Hawkes's canon after 1964, lingering on in a secondary role as emblematic of the past? Probably because when Hawkes finished *The Lime Twig* he knew that people have a Life-Force (Eros) to oppose their Death-Force (Thanatos), something he had perceived only dimly and expressed only intermittently before. Thus, during his next novel, *Second Skin*, lovescapes counterbalance warscapes, for by themselves the latter could no longer provide sufficient ambivalence.

This ambivalence about the unconscious created a paradoxical world where negative impulses lay behind positive actions and vice versa. Like complexity has never characterized Hawkes's view of the conscious mind, however. From *Charivari* on, consciousness helps make unconsciousness imaginative, dream visionary, molding chaotic images into controlled art. Ironically, then, an author often taken as a spokesman for the irrational guides his readers toward the rational. His landscapes are not mental transcriptions but maps.

At the widow's boardinghouse in *The Lime Twig*, Michael Banks's sexual fantasies, culminating in the arrival of the girl next door, are realized. He is drunk on love and liquor, and his internal disorder would seem to be reflected by the messy, noisy ambience there. Light conveys the atmosphere of the various rooms and situations he encounters: moonlight for Sybilline's bedroom, orange hallway light for the widow's sleeping chamber, lamplight for the parlor, car light for the pantry. Furniture and decorations of a brothel-like elegance—carved post, beaded glass shades, mauve velvet armchairs, portrait, candelabra, piano, cushions, carpeting, love seat—are also appropriate to an inebriated, orgiastic condition.

Queried about the widow's boardinghouse scene, Hawkes said it was not "a realistic representation of the character's distorted state of mind" since he was "not interested in portraying the psychic states of characters." Rather, such scenes convey "terrifying familiarity and unfamiliarity . . . controlled chaos" and are the "reality" emerging from "authorial visions" (Interview). Although the reader, recalling other episodes from *The Lime Twig* (and *The Blood Oranges*) might nevertheless insist that Hawkes employs expressionism, he should consider this refutation, for to Hawkes authorial domination is all important. Even during his psychodramas both inner and outer existences project the collective unconscious as transmitted by him.

At bottom non-realistic, non-surrealistic, non-expressionistic, Hawkes endows archetypical landscapes with *symbolic* settings. These form patterns to illuminate the world his people inhabit, a world that lacks stability. Change, isolation, and cheapness mark boardinghouses, hotels, and motels, where people come and go aimlessly, suffering loneliness, perversion, and violence. Impermanent homes, the result of a life-denying past, produce bad marriages, victimized children. Institutions tend to be transient, solitary affairs incapable of reducing tension. And aberrations flourish in public places, notably the nightclub/dance hall/restaurant, whose dance ritual dramatizes deviant sexual behavior.

The widow's boardinghouse is only one among several boardinghouses. The Bankses' boardinghouse is another. It symbolizes mutability. When lodger Hencher returns, the premises have altered—"an electric buzzer at the door, three flats instead of beds," "fresh paint, fresh window glass, new floorboards"—though to Hencher the place seems unchanged. He considers it "home" because his mother died there and he thinks "how permanent some transients are at last." But right after he takes possession he dies. Then thugs smash these quarters so that nothing remains: "Bare walls, bare floors, four empty rooms containing no scrap of paper, no figured piece of jewelry or elastic garment, no handwriting specimen by which the identity of the former occupants could be known."

Equally revealing is the boardinghouse that Stella runs

in *The Cannibal*. She lives on the street floor, while Balamir has the cellar, the Duke the second floor, the Census-Taker the third, Herr Stintz the fourth, and her sister and two children the fifth. Although lives cross, such an arrangement emphasizes the essential isolation of each. Their transiency extends to the setting itself. Downstairs Balamir cannot recover past furnishings, and upstairs the silver and glassware have become tarnished and dusty. Halls no longer smell of roasted pig, no longer ring with weighty laughter; they are cold, dark, streaked. If Zizendorf succeeds, the boardinghouse, once the "temporary seat of American representation," will change again into the National Headquarters. Some rooms would become a stenographic bureau and need additional windows. Already Stella's now clean and whitewashed chicken coop has been made Zizendorf's printing office.

Lonely, cheap, ominous hotels/motels characterized by sex and death recur too, most graphically perhaps in *Second Skin*. Protagonist-narrator Skipper tells his daughter, Cassandra, that her mother, Gertrude, wished to die among unmarried couples in a cheap motel and that he permitted it. At the U-Drive Inn, location of Gertrude's infidelities and binges, she suffers a solitude evidenced through pathetic mementos like pink mules, cuticle sticks, and dark glasses. Her son-in-law, Fernandez, lives close by at Tenochtitlan Trailer Village among mobile homes. Later, Skipper discovers him horribly mutilated in a Second Avenue flophouse no less shabby than his own hotel facing the Greyhound Terminal. Here an adolescent scrubwoman guards his daughter and granddaughter while they sleep on the thirteenth floor of this "place for suicide."

Honeymoon Hide-Away, the hotel where Cassandra and Fernandez spend their wedding night, rises from a ruined mining town whose barrenness makes Skipper feel trapped. Outside he smells "the rank odor of dead enterprise"; inside he connects death with sex. The hotel, formerly a call house, displays a cash register that resembles some "medieval machine of death." A bas-relief of naked Victorian females and an obsolete girlie calendar reflect the decadence of the hotel's rotten, rat-infested interior. Just prior to the wedding supper—a "tortured chicken skewered and brown and lacerated"—Fernandez calls Cassandra "Chicken." After supper, while the groom serenades the bride, Skipper becomes sick. Then he visits "another house of pleasure," the wasted opera hall. There he imagines the proprietress's thigh being caressed, orchestras, applause, and chorus girls. There he finds tickets for a movie starring Rita Hayworth as the unfaithful mistress of a jealous killer."

Traumatized, made impotent by his father's suicide during Skipper's childhood, Skipper makes such connections between sex and death throughout *Second Skin*. The undertaking parlor where he was raised, like most Hawkes homes, fostered a bad marriage and a victimized youngster.

In *The Cannibal* the house where Stella and Jutta grow up is "an old trunk covered with cracked sharkskin, heavier on top than the bottom, sealed with iron cornices and covered with shining fins." This selfish, secret, monstrous edifice also holds a querulous nurse, a pair of mad brothers, a senile father, and a bedridden mother. Both parents finally die, enabling Stella and Ernst to elope. When she returns, her home, which symbolizes past insularity and tyranny, looms "larger, darker, more out of date, more boarded up, than ever."

The house has a different, though equally disastrous impact on each girl. Stella, who was an adult in World War I, must uphold family tradition as Queen Mother. Jutta, who was still a juvenile during the war, must rebel. The younger sister feels malice toward the older and nothing whatsoever toward their mother and father. The father wanted her to be a civil servant, but she chose to be an architect, then entered the Saint Glauze nunnery.

Insecure homes are epitomized by vehicles that become habitations. One is the "salt and iron house" or beached sweeper Sparrow occupies in "A Little Bit of the Old Slap and Tickle"; another is "the traveling house" or red wagon Cap Leech practices from in *The Beetle Leg*. This wagon is "a cramped and wandering hovel," "a hut on wheels." With its disparate parts, it has the same makeshift look that the sweeper has. And, like Sparrow, Leech, prototypical roving quack, treasures his place. Even when not habitations, mechanical conveyances (cars, motorcycles, trucks, trains, buses, planes, boats) recur to supply rootless and restless movement.

Transient quarters, such as jails and hospitals, add to the insecure residence pattern. An ordered institution before, disorder descends on *The Cannibal*'s asylum during wartime. Harmonious buildings and meticulous underground networks, previously awesome, become "haphazard . . . out of all order . . . chaotic." Thieves destroy a sign bearing "the haven word 'asylum,' " and the institution ceases being a sanctuary. Order returns, but only temporarily. When the war ends, officials and nurses free their patients and depart. Subsequently, the latter chase livestock or crowd around fires. Then Zizendorf proclaims liberation and, full of public spirit, they file back. This new order will not endure, however, since Zizendorf, who favors a sadistic homosexual for Chancellor and an impotent drunkard for Secretary of State, is as demented as Balamir, who becomes his analogue just as the asylum becomes Germany's. Its warped citizens are imprisoned in an isolated and precarious country.

Another *Cannibal* setting shows that religious institutions are insecure too. In the time between her morbid home and a sordid boardinghouse, Jutta—bitter, ill, and defiant—dwells at the secluded nunnery, which perpetuates old familial pressures. World War I has been brought inside by a new director just off active duty. Whereas he is merely lustful, the Mother-Superior embodies the domination, insensitivity, and neglect characteristic of Jutta's parents. This new adult tyrant detests childish ragamuffins, yet the girl stands up to her, becoming especially uncooperative over confession. Jutta remains at Saint Glauze "alone, more silent, colder than ever."

Sequestered settings—graveyards, swamps, beaches, islands, and deserts—permeate Hawkes's work. So do public places people visit briefly: train and bus stations, streets and squares, resorts and gardens, stables and lavatories. Among them, the nightclub/dance hall/restaurant kind of establishment appears most often. All of Europe (Czechs, Poles, Belgians, Russians, Italians) gather in the storehouse adjoining the asylum during *The Cannibal* to dance, women with women, men with men. Appropriately, they mumble *"krank"* (sick), for they symbolize the sexual aberrations characteristic of the entire Occident. Such scenes are not uncommon: there is also the homosexual dancing at the *Caffè Gatto* (Cat or Tomcat) in *The Goose on the Grave,* for example.

This world functions on a more or less unconscious level too. Its quality of public nightmare resembles private nightmare as described by Ernest Jones in *On the Nightmare.* His "three cardinal features"—"agonizing dread," "suffocating sense of oppression," and "conviction of helpless paralysis"—define both. Hawkes has moved steadily away from the supernatural, but even in the later work may be found witch-like women, devil-like men. Other phenomena common to nightmare and superstition also recur. *On the Nightmare* cites:

the sudden transformation of one person into another or into some animal; the occurrence of phantastic and impossible animal forms; the alternation of the imagined object between extreme attractiveness and the most intense disgust; the apparently simultaneous existence of the same person in two different places; the idea of flying or riding through the air; and the apprehension of sexual acts as torturing assaults.

Jones claims that "*an attack of the Nightmare is an expression of a mental conflict over an incestuous desire.*" [6] It might seem far-fetched to call incest a major preoccupation in Hawkes's writing, since he "hadn't thought much about incest" and "incest doesn't mean as much to me as . . . to Faulkner" (Interview). The greater the conflict between wish and will, however, the more distorted the dream; and nightmare, enacting the unthinkable, conveys extreme dream-distortion. Though not consummated except in "The Traveler" and "The Grandmother," where Justus Kümmerlich has a child by his brother's wife, incestuous feelings pervade the Hawkes canon. Often those involved are actually related, but sometimes they are related only on a symbolic level. Incestuous feelings between fathers and daughters are hinted at in *Charivari, The Cannibal, The Owl, Second Skin,* and *The Questions,* while incestuous feelings between mothers and sons are suggested in *Charivari, The Beetle Leg,* and *The Lime Twig.* Between brothers and sisters these feelings appear in *The Lime Twig* and *The Innocent Party.*

Incest seems to be a central motif in three of six full-length novels: *The Beetle Leg, The Lime Twig* and *Second Skin.* It is significant that Hawkes's protagonist in *The Lime*

*Twig*, Michael Banks, bears the name of the brother in the Mary Poppins series, for he unconsciously regards his wife as his sister. It is also significant that the book focuses on the horse, Rock Castle, since, according to Jones, a horse is the dominant nightmare symbol, combining attraction and repulsion, Eros and Thanatos. Michael's "own worse dream, and best" concerns Rock Castle, the possession of which leads to an orgy with Margaret's alter-ego, the gun-moll Sybilline. When Michael's erotic feelings over his wife-sister surface at the racetrack, he stops Rock Castle but the latter crushes him. During an earlier, parallel incident, the horse also trampled Hencher, who had harbored obvious incestuous desires toward his "mother." Crushing and trampling are appropriate actions because they simultaneously signify sexual intercourse and its punishment.

On a more or less unconscious level, then, such public nightmares contain the principal phenomena, the mental conflict, and the dominant symbol Jones discerns in private nightmares. The author's world therefore has psychoanalytic validity and carries the reader beyond outer actuality to inner reality, an inner reality whose instability is symbolized by Hawkes's landscapes and settings.

Hawkes creates atmosphere through locations that recur and meaning by juxtaposing these locations. One juxtaposition, involving civilization and nature, goes back at least to the Renaissance. As industrialization and urbanization grew, this juxtaposition became more and more common. It pitted rural virtues against urban evils in eighteenth- and nineteenth-century novels like *Tom Jones* and *Great Expectations,* which take young men on educational journeys from country to town to country. Although not quite so pervasive during the twentieth-century, the pro-nature, anti-civilization bias continues. For example,

Hemingway's protagonists, who are the product of a romantic sensibility too, understand what Tom and Pip learned: nature is good, civilization bad. Jakes Barnes in *The Sun Also Rises* flees Pamplona, where he played the pimp, and goes fishing with Bill Gorton at Burguete, where he plays the sportsman. A sanctuary, nature restores him.

Other twentieth-century writers invert the traditional position. In Sartre's *La Nausée*, Roquentin comments:

I am afraid of cities. But you mustn't leave them. If you go too far you come up against the vegetation belt. Vegetation has crawled for miles toward the cities. It is waiting. Once the city is dead, the vegetation will cover it, will climb over the stones, grip them, search them, make them burst with its long black pincers; it will blind the holes and let its green paws hang over everything. You must stay in the cities as long as they are alive, you must never penetrate along this great mass of hair waiting at the gates; you must let it undulate and crack all by itself. In the cities, if you know how to take care of yourself, and choose the times when all the beasts are sleeping in their holes and digesting, behind the heaps of organic debris, you rarely come across anything more than minerals, the least frightening of all existants.[7]

Through an emphasis on physical reality and cosmic absurdity, Hawkes bears some semblance to the existentialists, so it is not surprising that his view of nature recalls Roquentin's. Hawkes, however, never makes the town a refuge from the country, which suggests one of several fundamental philosophical differences. For Sartre, existence precedes essence, but for Hawkes, whose pre-1960 work is clearly deterministic, essence precedes existence. Existential gestures like Michael Banks's suicide seldom appear in the work of a man quoted as calling evil "one of the pure words I mean to preserve." [8]

Hawkes's attitude toward both human nature and external nature reflects an affinity with the pessimistic puritanical school of Melville and Hawthorne rather than the optimistic transcendental school of Emerson and Thoreau. Among the recent American writers he respects, Djuna Barnes, Flannery O'Connor, and Nathanael West best represent this darker position. His own early negative attitude receives fullest and deepest expression in *The Beetle Leg*, partly through the apposition of town and country settings.

The towns of Mistletoe and Clare, twenty miles apart, are juxtaposed to their respective surroundings, a river and a desert. Mistletoe, the horseshoe town with horseshoe windows, exhibits neither luck nor those positive properties of healing, sacredness, protection, and revelation Sir James G. Frazer attributed to its parasitic namesake. Like Clare, whose jail figures prominently amid a few drab buildings and people, Mistletoe is just another small western village containing brown houses, Estrellita's drug store, and the Metal and Lumber Gymnasium. Beyond Clare lies the desert, which the Sheriff warns about: "A man is wise if he keeps to town." Beyond Mistletoe are the river, dam, mountain, and badlands. Mulge Lampson was buried in the dam and his mother—Mistletoe's "first natural death"—on the bluff above. Their environment is airless and even the fishing is bad.

The desert has obliterated all traces of previous human existence, including, perhaps, nomad tribes and tended fields. Under the river are forsaken townsites of unrecorded communities—Fat Chance, Reshuffle, Dynamite —still remembered by some nearby residents. Water is as treacherous as sand: the Sheriff drags the river; Luke Lampson hooks an infant corpse at the bottleneck. Later, he and two others occupy a boat, which has survived the disappearance of the great forks. It capsizes, but before doing so it strikes an empty house—the drowned farm Cap Leech equates with Eden. The house's windows are closed and its contents placed in a tree, yet these precautions against flooding have proved futile, for water, like sand, inevitably annihilates man and his world.

Inspired by the phenomenon of the hill easing "down the rotting shale a beetle's leg each several anniversaries," the title suggests the notion of irresistible force. More than this hill shifts. Water is pushing the dam gulfward, and fissures spreading along the land to trap mice and lizards will crack open someday and destroy a decade of work. Although Clare escaped Mistletoe's Great Slide, external nature nonetheless diminishes it, for "The silent flatlands, the lonely shrubs, the plains, moved in upon the town and passed across the weeded railroad line, carrying part of Clare off into the night."

Former inhabitant Camper returns to the Mistletoe region and immediately encounters natural noxiousness. While Camper's car lights illuminate a poisoned water sign, Luke, who has never suffered from snakebite on his infested range but who has witnessed other peoples' susceptibility, cures the bitten Camper child. Mosquitoes (and blister beetles) are present too: when Luke treats the child, they bite the father, and, when the father greets Luke at the Buckhouse, they cling to the shade.

People share a similar noxiousness. Leech's hands, despite disinfectants and rubber gloves, are covered with small warts, and Ma's arm develops an annoying sore that she tends as faithfully as Luke lances or cauterizes pit viper wounds. The Finn is a crippled ex-bronc rider, underweight and dependent on braces and crutches; his companion, Harry Bohn—"by miracle born of a dead mother"—is senile at the age of thirty. And, no matter how much the

Metal and Lumber workers immerse their feet to control fungus, they become reimpregnated every morning from flaking skin and discharge.

The Sheriff's opening remark, "It is a lawless country," indicates that people have psychic disorders too. The Red Devil motorcycle gang exhibits criminal behavior. These creatures, who are associated with animals, form a herd and so possess snouts and claws. They seem "jerkined Indians" at one point, an allusion of some significance since the Mandan and other Indians recur to make tacit comments on the white man's savagery. But whether non-human and mechanical or human and uncontrollable, the fiendish Red Devils participate in the victimizer-turned-victim theme, which Hawkes develops by terming them hunters, then prey. What they actually do—scratch up a dog, shatter a window, interrupt a dance, practice voyeurism, steal apples—hardly justifies their becoming the target of shotguns.

The posse or victims-turned-victimizers are instinctual hunters, as the imagery during the Sheriff's ambush demonstrates. He, Bohn, and Luke approach the Red Devils with fingers that itch and lips that taste fur. The conflict concludes when Luke, whose weapon has backfired, reverts to a more primitive, brutal state:

And suddenly, from the isolated battering truck, shrill and buoyant above the clumsiness of thick-kneed marksmen, there came that cool baying of the rising head, the call to kill, louder and singsong, faintly human after the flight of Devils, the nasal elated sounds of the cowboy's western bark.

Yip, yip, yip.

Mock battles reveal how public aggression and mass psychic disorder stem from erotic sources. The warring factions in *The Beetle Leg*, no less than in *The Cannibal* where Stella's females crush the asylum's males, are sexually distorted. "Sleek black gas tanks" brace the crotches of the androgynous Red Devils. Among those originally pursuing them, Camper alone is married, but he soon abandons his jealous wife. Her promiscuous rival loves Bohn vainly, since Bohn, like the Sheriff, prefers male companionship and "the expressionless genitals of animals." Luke remains celibate throughout. When he, Bohn, and the Sheriff shoot rock salt at their antagonists' buttocks. Hawkes reiterates the connection between violence and sex introduced earlier during the chase. Then Bohn felt a "satisfied warning in his groin."

Neither external nature nor human nature appears to be governable. Man cannot harness the first by machinery—the Great Slide took place—nor can he civilize himself by technological improvements. Mistletoe-Clare will never furnish a viable alternative to river-desert.

That death-driven external nature and human nature are interrelated forces is demonstrated in the futile and tainted efforts of two analogous characters equally concerned about noxious growth. Leech's name and the Sheriff's title establish their complete identification with medicine man and law man. For thirty years, Leech has been practicing among hopeless patients; for fourteen, the Sheriff has been patrolling still lawless country. Leech, who enjoys surgery, works from a red wagon (hospital), where he burns "powders to kill disease." The Sheriff, who enjoys "the extra weight of a gun and the sound of a closing door," operates from a jail, where he *temporarily* restrains felons like the Red Devils.

These men represent more than dedicated ineffectiveness. Supposedly custodians of personal and social soundness, they are really quacks, one an unlicensed

doctor-dentist, the other a superstitious law officer. Both
participate in the corruption ascribed to external nature
and human nature, as Leech's warts signify. Father of Luke
and Mulge, this irresponsible, lecherous old man deserts
their mother, then, later, mock-rapes their ward, the Mandan. While extracting her tooth, he becomes frustrated
over her "Indian pap," "violet pudendum" and "raised
skirt"—an unconscious reaction which leads him to slay a
rooster. The rooster is called "squatting quarry" and she
"captive," so they symbolize the prey of the doctor no less
than the Red Devils symbolize the prey of the Sheriff,
whose cry, "Kill most anything tonight," sums up his own
sick soul. Though Hawkes alludes only to Leech in direct
Adamic terms, nearly all *The Beetle Leg* characters share
Adamic frailty. For example, "Physician, heal thyself!"
could be aimed at Luke too, since, unlike the New Testament evangelist Luke, he inflicts as well as cures wounds.

The identification established here and throughout
the canon between external nature and human nature
echoes the Medieval-Renaissance doctrine of correspon-
dences, not the dichotomous view of later centuries.
Hawkes's attitude toward external nature and human nature changes after 1960, but their parallel noxiousness and
uncontrollability in his fiction persist. Skipper, the protagonist of *Second Skin,* while embodying Eros, also embodies Thanatos; furthermore, on his paradisiacal Floating
Island there is a swamp associated with foul odors, frightful
sounds, grotesque animal and plant life, danger, and extinction. Hawkes, who discovers paradox everywhere, once
said this later novel concealed barbs under its blossoms.

In *The Lime Twig,* which is concluded by the first effec-
tive life-oriented action Hawkes created—Michael stopping
Rock Castle out of love for Margaret—external nature appears indifferent rather than hostile. Not until after *The*

*Lime Twig* are the Life-Force and Death-Force sufficiently defined to create sustained conflict. When they are, the novels become more dramatic, since their author always projects thought through technique. His settings consequently acquire greater structural importance in *Second Skin* and *The Blood Oranges*, where, however complicated, place, like character, tends to represent either Eros or Thanatos.

# 2

# Myths and Rituals

Skipper's phrase for the Atlantic island, "my mythic rock," echoes Hawkes's phrase, "my 'mythic' England, Germany, Italy, American west, tropical island, and so on," [9] and suggests that Hawkesian settings are as invented, imaginary, and fictitious as Hawkesian landscapes. Of these settings, the primordial one symbolizing paradise lost seems most important. Opposed to the New England Atlantic island is the Caribbean Floating Island. Though paradisiacal, it contains an ominous swamp where Skipper strives vainly to remove an iguana from the back of his mistress, Catalina Kate. Comparable watery places associated with corpses and serpents recur throughout the fiction. Two bear the name "Eden." One, the setting of *The Innocent Party*, deteriorates from "obsolescence and rank decay," but water is nevertheless important as a dry swimming pool fills up when the protagonist chooses her lascivious aunt over her inhibited parents who are terrorized daily by a centipede combining serpentine and satanic traits. And the other, the setting of *The Beetle Leg*, brings together water, corpses, snakes, and devils.

Settings and landscapes are not the only aspects of Hawkes's work affected by the use of legend. Mythological elements drawn from contemporary, pagan, and Judaic-Christian sources also provided tone, characterization, action, and meaning.

The comic tone of *The Beetle Leg* and *The Lime Twig* was set when Hawkes began to parody conventional novels and their treatment of modern myths. *The Beetle Leg* takes a derisive attitude toward the American western, and *The Lime Twig* a derisive attitude toward the crime thriller. Parody ridicules formal aspects of fiction: during *The Lime Twig* one narrator's language exposes journalistic cheapness, and another's death violates narrative expectation. Both books go beyond parody, however, to burlesque, which ridicules the spirit or aim of the original, and to travesty, which ridicules its nobility or dignity.

*The Beetle Leg* mocks the popular conception of the American West, achieving comedy through exaggerated characters and situations. Extreme literary stereotypes, *all* the women are betrayed. Ma, a pioneer woman inseparable from an enormous deep dish skillet, and Lou, a sophisticated outsider possessing perfume, slacks, and diamonds, undertake parallel searches for faithless husbands. Hattie, a deserted frontier mother, cuts off both sons prior to her death and afterwards dominates one son from her gravesite. Thegna, the Norwegian cook, loves unrequitedly the asexual Bohn. Maverick, the Mandan, suffers symbolic rape at the hands of sadistic Cap Leech. Other actions magnify their isolation: Lou confronts Thegna over her errant husband, then joins a card game that should involve men but involves four companionless old lady cardsharps instead. At the same time, the men, representing extreme literary stereotypes too, are *all* impotent. There are two major factions. The first is the Sheriff's posse and includes a devoted deputy, a senile misogynist, a celibate cowboy, a crippled ex-bronc rider, a lecherous quack-doctor, and a boyish greenhorn. The posse tracks down the second group, a hermaphroditic motorcycle band who caricature outlaws and Indians by committing innocuous crimes. During the ambush, comic exaggeration culminates when the posse fires rock salt into the buttocks of these "cornered apple thieves."

Another modern myth, the crime thriller, is used in *The Lime Twig*,[10] which mocks underworld events by making them inordinately sensational: the trampling of Hencher, the drugging of Sparrow, the threatening, seducing, and crushing of Michael, the smashing of the flat, the slitting of Cowles's throat, the beating and raping of Margaret, the shooting of Monica. Inexplicable things often occur to subvert the logic that characterizes detective fiction. Annie, "a girl [Michael] had seen through windows in several dreams unremembered," appears without explanation at the widow's parlor, where she makes love to him and enigmatically warns him against Hencher. Then at the paddock she kisses a jockey she scarcely knows.

Almost as outrageous as the events are the criminals, victims and law officers of *The Lime Twig*. The criminals include Larry, the head mobster, Sparrow and Thick, his henchmen, and Little Dora and Sybilline, his molls. The henchmen and molls are absurdly opposite pairs. Sparrow and Thick caricature the small, defective bodyguard serving out of gratitude and the gross, brutal executioner hired for money. When unpredictable Larry chooses Little Dora over her sister Sybilline, proposing, "A bit of marriage, eh?" he unaccountably selects the old and the ugly over the young and the beautiful. *Lime Twig* victims, though familiar, are excessively helpless—innocent females, obese males—as *Lime Twig* law officers, also familiar, are excessively incompetent. Such characters deride their mythic counterparts.

Many Hawkes people bear mythological epithets or become associated with mythological figures. Among the latter, three biblical personages—Mary, Satan, and Christ—frequently recur.

Mary lends her name to promiscuous Cassandra of *Second Skin*, whose incestuous father calls the girl "BVM" (Blessed Virgin Mary) and whose homosexual husband owns a "tall white plastic Madonna"; to licentious Bianca Maria of *The Goose on the Grave;* to *Santa Maria,* the ship that sensual Phoebe of *The Innocent Party* takes around the world. When not ironically implying wantonness, Mary ironically implies weakness. This latter quality pervades *The Owl,* where the Donna or white statue and the gallows or tall lady are juxtaposed.

Only *The Beetle Leg* Red Devils actually boast Satan's popular title, but other individuals represent him. In *The Cannibal,* Herr Snow emerges a "red-bearded devil" and Herr Stintz an "animal-devil"; in *Second Skin,* Sonny tells Skipper: "That devil [Tremlow] been the whole show, that's the devil got them stirred up this way." In *The Innocent Party,* Beatrix screams, "You devil!" at the sleeping Phoebe. Hawkes's greatest Satan, Larry, "is almost a god, a demonic god." [11]

The ambivalence attributed to these Satans and Antichrists also characterizes the Christ-figures, usually personified by children and child-like adults. One, the foreign prisoner of *The Owl,* slays four ganders, and another, Adeppi of *The Goose on the Grave,* leads an old man to his death. Such victimized scapegoats obviously share original sin.

Sometimes Hawkes constructs action along mythological lines. For example, the seduction of Michael by Sybilline during *The Lime Twig* recalls the Circe legend. In *The Greek Myths*, Robert Graves writes:

Circe sat in her hall, singing to her loom and, when Eurylochus's party raised a halloo, stepped out with a smile and invited them to dine at her table. All entered gladly, except Eurylochus himself who, suspecting a trap, stayed behind and peered anxiously in at the windows. The goddess set a mess of cheese, barley, honey, and wine before the hungry sailors; but it was drugged, and no sooner had they begun to eat than she struck their shoulders with her wand and transformed them into hogs. Grimly then she opened the wicket of a sty, scattered a few handfuls of acorns and cornel-cherries on the miry floor, and left them there to wallow.[12]

Elements from this myth are incorporated in the action of *The Lime Twig*, where there is no Eurylochus and where Circe becomes Sybilline (Cybele: mother of the gods; Sibyl: a prophetess). Michael, like Odysseus, is married, but unlike Odysseus, he does not acquire a charm to counteract the goddess's magic. As was the case with the hungry sailors, food, drink, and song accompany his enchantment and metamorphosis. He first sees Sybilline at the Pavillion, where he gulps down the gin she orders, then lets her lead him through the crowd. Next they are discovered at an Italian restaurant eating spaghetti, drinking wine, and dancing to romantic melodies. There, before she offers "lips soft, venereal, sweet and tasting of sex," Sybilline laughs, "We'll go to bed and you'll like my bed."

Food, drink, and song soon reappear at the widow's parlor to furnish the context for Michael's final transformation. "Drugged" now, he is the plaything of Sybilline, who says, "I've seduced you, haven't I," as he crawls after her lost pearls. Later, he swinishly devours the eggs she has cooked after her question, "Don't you know what eggs are good for?" Then, rubbing meat sauce against the widow, he believes these eggs "had done the job for him," implying that they have enabled him to copulate with the widow after three sessions with Sybilline-Circe. Subsequently, he continues to exhibit piggish behavior when copulating with Annie, an act also made possible by the aphrodisiac eggs.

During the same novel, Hawkes introduces the Icarus myth. Hencher's van and Larry's limousine have radiator caps decorated with "a winged man." Scalded and "in attitude of pursuit," one cap flies off, whereupon Hencher kicks it away. A general thematic parallel is established between the rebellious flight toward the sun and the consequent drowning of Icarus, on one hand, and, on the other, the rebellious flight toward "dream desires" and the consequent crushing of Michael.

A more comprehensive use of mythology, providing landscape/setting, tone, characterization, action, and meaning simultaneously, appears in *Second Skin* and *The Beetle Leg*.

Myths of the Trojan War and of Shakespeare's *The Tempest* are interwoven in *Second Skin*. Skipper views himself as Menelaus, Priam, and Iphigenia. A childhood copybook contains the prophetic, trustful confession, *"I have soon to journey to a lonely island in a distant part of my kingdom. But I shall return before the winter storms begin. Prince Paris, I leave my wife, Helen, in your care. Guard her well. See that no harm befalls her."* The speaker here is certainly Menelaus and the journey probably his Cretan voyage, during which Helen and Paris eloped. Earlier, Skipper had noted, "Cassandra stood by watching, waiting, true to her name," a name that for Skipper apparently connotes prophetess. He may or may not grasp its other implications—unwed mother of Agamemnon's twin sons and victim of their murderers, Clytemnestra and Aegisthus—but as father to Cassandra he nonetheless be-

comes Priam. He becomes Iphigenia too, who he believes
was sacrificed by Agamemnon rather than saved by Artemis:

Had I been born my mother's daughter instead of son—and the
thought is not so improbable, after all, and causes me neither
pain, fear nor embarrassment when I give it my casual and
interested contemplation—I would not have matured into a muscular and self-willed Clytemnestra but rather into a large and
innocent Iphigenia betrayed on the beach. A large and slow-eyed
and smiling Iphigenia, to be sure, even more full to the knife than
that real girl struck down once on the actual shore. Yet I am
convinced that in my case I should have been spared.

Skipper's Floating Island in the West Indies (Grenada)
is reminiscent of Prospero's uninhabited island in the Ber-
mudas. Here Skipper was washed ashore, rejoining his
former mess boy and finding three new black disciples.
Their leader, he soon metamorphoses from Ariel to Prospero, though he dwells at a Plantation House instead of a
cell and practices artificial insemination instead of magic.
Miranda, the arch-enemy from whom he fled, bears her
Shakespearean counterpart's name:

I hear that name—Miranda, Miranda!—and once again quicken
to its false suggestiveness, feel its rhapsody of sound, the several
throbs of the vowels, the very music of charity, innocence, obedi-
ence, love. For a moment I seem to see both magic island and
imaginary girl. But Miranda was the widow's name—out of what
perversity, what improbable desire I am at a loss to say—and no
one could have given a more ugly denial to that heartbreaking
and softly fluted name than the tall and treacherous woman.

In his article "Necessary Landscapes and Luminous
Deteriorations," Tony Tanner is right to claim that Skipper

represents both Priam, the last king of Troy, and Prospero, the ruler of an enchanted isle, and therefore possesses *two* daughters (Cassandra *and* Miranda); but he is wrong when adding that these figures, since they "turned out so ironically different from their prototypes," show "how free Skipper feels he can be in his mythologizing." [13] Indeed, the father-daughter pattern dominates the Trojan War-*Tempest* reference throughout *Second Skin* and indicates that its apparently arbitrary allusions are carefully designed. Skipper identifies with Priam and Prospero because he considers them virtuous fathers deserted by promiscuous daughters. He identifies with Iphigenia because she represents a loving daughter sacrificed by a cruel father.

The theme of sexual betrayal, involving mothers and sons as well as husbands and wives and fathers and daughters, stems from the connection between Skipper's incestuous desires and his impotence. His impotence helps to make *Second Skin* a travesty of *The Tempest,* a travesty that begins when Skipper says, "I was tossed up spent and half-naked on the invisible shore of our wandering island—old Ariel in sneakers, sprite surviving in bald-headed man of fair complexion."

Although Shakespearean and Hawkesian island are alike in being geographically remote and psychologically fantastic, the Hawkesian Ariel caricatures the Shakespearean Ariel by his ridiculous, earthbound appearance. It is King Alonso's party that is "tossed up" in *The Tempest,* not the "ayrie spirit" that brings about their stormy predicament before rescuing them.

Travesty continues as Skipper becomes Prospero. The Duke practices an "Art," which, according to Frank Kermode, has two functions: "He exercises the supernatural powers of the holy adept," and "Prospero's Art controls

Nature." [14] Clearly, artificial insemination debases "super-natural powers" and the inseminator the adept. The second function fares no better. To Prospero, controlling nature means restraining sexual impulses, and he accordingly supervises the courtship of Ferdinand and Miranda. In Skipper such impulses have died, and his real son-in-law (homosexual) and symbolic daughter (fornicatress) are not present.

Like the interrelated Trojan war and _Tempest_ myths of _Second Skin_, the use of Osiris and Fisher King myths in _The Beetle Leg_ conveys landscape/setting, tone, characterization, action, and meaning concurrently.

The pagan Osiris myth and the Christian Fisher King myth are flood myths. About such myths, Mircea Eliade says: "The Jews held similar ideas—the loss of the original Paradise, the progressive shortening of the span of human life, the Flood that annihilated humanity except for a few privileged individuals." These flood myths, Eliade maintains, often mention "a ritual fault that aroused the wrath of the Supreme Being," [15] Consciously or not, Hawkes implies ritual fault as he creates paradise lost. In _The Innocent Party_, Jane discovers a sign reading COLORED ONLY when she arrives at the abandoned motel and keeps it. The ritual fault there, then, is the displacement of sexual, life-oriented blacks by sexless, death-oriented whites. In _The Beetle Leg_, Mulge's personal fault of marrying an elderly mother-surrogate becomes analogous to Mistletoe's communal fault of damming up the river, since both block natural forces. Jehova punishes Adam and Eve for their carnality, but Hawkes, who inverts original sin, punishes Mulge and Mistletoe for their sterility.

The corn-god Osiris was born from an adulterous intrigue between the Earth and the Sky. He wed a sister, Isis, and with her help civilized the cannibalistic Egyptians by

the introduction of grains. When he returned after spreading enlightenment elsewhere, a brother, Typhon, betrayed
him, sealing the twenty-eight-year-old king-god in a coffer
and flinging the coffer into the Nile. Then Isis "put on a
mourning attire, and wandered disconsolately up and
down, seeking the body." Osiris floated toward Syria; there,
at Byblus, the trunk of a tree closed round the coffer. Isis
removed the coffer, but Typhon proceeded to mutilate and
disperse the body. The fact that she buried the pieces as she
found them explains the god's many gravesites and relics.
Fish, however, had eaten his penis, so the corn-goddess
fashioned a replica. She and another sister, Nephthys,
composed an archetypal lament for their beneficent, true-
speaking brother, who became the mummified Ruler of the
Dead, promising everlasting life.[16] A number of references
enlarge this selective account of "The Myth of Osiris" in
subsequent chapters of *The Golden Bough:*

Thus Lactantius regarded Osiris as the son instead of the husband of Isis. . . .
   Further, the story that his mangled remains were scattered
up and down the land and buried in different places may be a
mythical way of expressing either the sowing or the winnowing of
the grain. . . .
   As a god of vegetation Osiris was naturally conceived as a god
of creative energy in general, since men at a certain stage of
evolution fail to distinguish between the reproductive powers of
animals and of plants. . . . [17]

   In *From Ritual to Romance*, which, like *The Golden Bough*,
influenced Hawkes's model, *The Waste Land*, lending it title,
plan, and symbolism, Jessie L. Weston sums up the most
relevant material on the Fisher King or the medieval Christian counterpart of such vegetation deities as Osiris:

(a) There is a general consensus of evidence to the effect that the main object of the Quest is the restoration to health and vigour of a King suffering from infirmity caused by wounds, sickness, or old age;

(b) and whose infirmity, for some mysterious and unexplained reason, reacts disastrously upon his kingdom, either depriving it of vegetation, or exposing it to the ravages of war. . . .

(d) In both cases where we find Gawain as the hero of the story, and in one connected with Perceval, the misfortune which has fallen upon the country is that of a prolonged drought, which has destroyed vegetation, and left the land waste; the effect of the hero's question is to restore the waters to their channel, and render the land once more fertile.

The Fisher King, whose name signifies "origin and preservation of Life" and whose role combines Godhead and kingship, usually dies and is then mourned by Weeping Women. Figuratively castrated for a sexual sin, his lost virility, through sympathetic magic, induces corresponding infertility in external nature. Neither he nor the land can be vivified until the Quester poses the right question and occasions the freeing of the waters. Miss Weston feels that the Quester may represent another figure, "the Doctor, or Medicine Man, . . . no unimportant link in the chain which connects these practices with the Grail tradition." [18]

In *The Beetle Leg* many references establish the mythic stature of Mulge. When Lou inquiries about her husband Camper, the welders' perversely ironic responses confuse him and Mulge. Speculation about where "he" might go leads to the following exchange:

"They'd riot again if he come back."
"That's right, after all we mourned."
. . . "Not every town would make as much of him as us."

Before somebody protests, "Lady, don't ask us any more," somebody else answers, "He'd be forty years old now . . . and not liked near so well." The answer, putting Mulge around Jesus' age when the Great Slide occurred, precedes an Old Testament allusion:

    "Jonah."
    . . . "Except if it had been a whale, he might have escaped."

"Awed with the knell of the one death," an accident which "had rocked the little purgatory," the welders comment: "In those days you could have followed him down the street"; "And if he stopped, you could have touched him"; "It was hard to believe he was gone"; "Turned his back on us." Their assertion, "We ain't forgot," concludes the scene.

But Mulge is more than a local legend with sporadic mythological associations, for his fate burlesques that of Osiris and the Fisher King. Conceived during an adulterous liaison between Hattie Lampson and Cap Leech, their son, Mulge, dies at about thirty, though not from wounds or sickness. Brother Luke's hostility toward him resembles Typhon's toward Osiris, but Mulge dies accidentally, not by fratricide. Both are trapped in water—the king-god above, the anti-king-god below—and both are buried in doubtful graves. Mulge is neither resurrected like Osiris-Christ nor restored like the Fisher King. Anything but a vegetation deity, he bears no sexual wound, lies in a grave that takes "seeding badly," and leaves secular relics (shoes, razor, shaving mug, septic pencil, postcards, photographs) very different from the religious relics (backbone, head, phallic images) left by Osiris. Nonetheless, he shares the ritual fault of such deities. As Osiris married Isis (sister, mother), Mulge marries his surrogate-mother Ma; then, on their honeymoon, he abandons her and his real mother Hattie for the previously deceived Thegna. "No one ever even thought they had done one thing to shame us, at least not before the older married," says the Sheriff. Hawkes emphasizes this shame, this sexual crime, when he reveals that "Ma was already old when she married" and that she was accompanied across the desert by several ancient females wishing "to see one woman their own age brought to bed."

Mulge debases the mythical water-god; and Ma, who wears "black summer or winter" and "actively pined away and opened many graves to find one full," debases the Weeping Women. A divining rod leads her over "sacred ground," as she cries, "Oh, Mulge. Where are you, Mulge?" on a search which is as much travesty as the ceremonial marriage and rites involving water, Tarot pack, and Medicine Man. The medicine men in *The Beetle Leg,* Leech and Luke, have become the reverse of healers like Gawain. Nor do Luke and Camper make successful fishermen, the first catching only a dead baby and the second nothing at all. Ironically, these questers never ask the right question, and the waters are freed to produce Eliade's annihilative rather than Weston's restorative flood. Her Messianic Fish-Meal will not be served.

Hawkes has remarked, "It's paradoxical that someone who knows as little about the Bible as I do nonetheless uses some of these materials" (Interview). Paradoxical or not, religious materials permeate his work from start to finish, as a savage indictment of Christianity.

During the early *Goose on the Grave,* Adeppi, the boy protagonist, encounters Brothers Dolce and Bolo. The first is obsessed by Christ's face and behaves masochistically, and the second practices simony. In the novitiate these frustrated celibates stitch rat skins about an old woman;

afterward they abduct and burn Adeppi's mother. He manages to find a surrogate-mother, barren Arsella, but she occupies quarters adorned with "a bleeding heart" and encourages sexual intimacies that lead to his involvement in her blind husband's murder. The boy fares no better from Christian groups than from Christian individuals. A congregation attending church ignores Adeppi's cries when a soldier pummels him, and another congregation shouts, "O sacrilegio, sacrilegio!" when he flees Dolce.

Though less blatant, this negative attitude toward Christianity continues throughout the post-1960 fiction. In "The Nearest Cemetery," the short story that was the basis for *Second Skin*, the narrator-barber mentions "a shingled church with windows as bright and painful as some of my own dreams." Eventually he adds, mentioning his fanatical wife, "The barber cannot bear to listen to Mildred pumping and marching with the Lord at the town's church organ. The Lord and Mildred deafen me." Skipper, like the barber, finds both church and believers sinister. References to the first are expanded during *Second Skin* by the Gentle Island portions, where Lutheran Church and Puritan graves appear. His betrayers have religious affiliations: Bubbles "must surely be the daughter of the frenzied sexton," while Miranda, Captain Red, Jomo, and Bub meet over "midday dinners on the Sabbath"—"the dangerous day of the Lord." In general, *Second Skin*'s Protestants, with their "sour souls . . . poke bonnets . . . sunken . . . accusing horse faces and dreary choruses," form an unflattering contrast to its Catholics. Indeed, Mac, the Catholic chaplain, saves Skipper, and he is served by Sonny, whose hatband bears "bright paper medallions of the Roman Church." This is deceptive, however, since corrupt Fernandez is Skipper's "little old-world Catholic son-in-law." He not only possesses a Madonna, but classifies silver as "the precious metal of the church, the metal of devotion, ceremony, candlelight." Even Skipper's innocent disciple, Sister Josie, becomes "a thin devoted example of missionary madness."

With the exception of actions involving the cross, Hawkes treats religious rituals as negative. Near the end of *The Cannibal* there can be heard "the faraway scraping of knives and forks," signaling that the Duke and Stella have begun the meal he prepared the previous evening. One of the courses is a broth made from human flesh and served with wine, echoing the Eucharist. About pursuing and eating their victim, Hawkes admitted: "These are pretty perverse rituals throughout rather than the constructive life-producing rituals." [19] The pursuit of Jutta's boy by the Duke is as ritualistic as this black Communion: it involves a hunter stalking, slaying, skinning, and dissecting a "young and frightened fox." The fox hunt in the play *The Questions* also connects sex and violence with sacrificial rites. Papa, formerly a Charleston aristocrat and a Master of Hounds but now an impotent cuckold, joins Mama's English lover for "the sacrifice." During the mutilation ceremony, he claims "they were all Mau-Maus at heart," and the lover throws Mama "some bloody appendage" (possibly a penis), shouting, "Here you go, mother, catch," which she does. Earlier, Mama was called "some dark huntsman from another age."

Designated "judgment supper," *The Owl*'s more extended ceremonial dinner takes place in a senatorial chamber, where a hangman whose totem is *Il Gufo* (The Owl), sits at table "under the tester blazoned with the escutcheon of a burst fess, a black leathern tapestry . . . reputed to have once been the skirt of a barbarian conqueror," flanked by twelve Monger-apostles. What Miss Weston describes as the Messianic Fish-Meal displaces the bread and wine of the Last Supper and the paschal lamb of the Passover. Signor Barado-Judas—a name suggesting Barabas—betrays the hangman-Antichrist when he pleads for the prisoner-Christ, and he betrays the prisoner-Christ when he signs "the Death Decree." Hawkes asserts, "The judgment supper was served . . . food . . . to bind the officials to the hangman and to perpetuate the feast of the law body which preceded Sasso Fetore's original compulsory execution." Although the apostles could hardly be considered officials or law body, there are some clear parallels between judgment supper and Last Supper. Christ's disciples were also bound through food (bread = body, wine = blood), and this Communion was also perpetuated. An execution also succeeds the biblical feast, though victim rather than victimizer presides. Because Hawkes's judgment supper celebrates death, it inverts both life-giving Eucharist and Messianic Fish-Meal.

The behavior of these participants illustrates how automatically and obsessively Hawkes's characters act out perverted religious rituals. Dressed alike, the Mongers exhibit "traditional magisterial ruffs" and gavels. The hangman eats with "a three-tined fork and a dull knife," but the Mongers must pick up with their fingers the oily fish ("fare of all the verdicts delivered") which have given them their title. When Signor Barabo breaks the "period for silence," the hangman raps the table and passes the knife before his face twice, "blade toward the lips." Soon the hunchback who is methodically collecting the thirteen porcelain platters taps every diner except the hangman "so that the citizen should be represented" and "fraternal feelings . . . expressed." Later: "The first man to rise, rip open his hempen shirt, and expose his breast was allowed to speak, the rest thereafter not needing to perform this ritual." Because he desperately wants a husband for his daughter,

Signor Barabo shows both chest and belly as he begs the tribunal to grant the prisoner a white card of innocence, which the hangman refuses, observing that "these old masters . . . sentenced not a few." The prisoner is no exception:

> How long shall be the length of rope? That was decided.
> And the braid of the rope, fine or coarse? That was decided.
> Was blood to be drawn first from the throat or not? That was decided.
> And who shall be witness? Also decided.

Once the hunchback has provided each Monger with a quill and some writing fluid (ash and water), they draft "the Death Decree" containing the condemned's name. Then the oligarchy, turning their backs on oil paintings of their predecessors, trails the hangman from "the only white building in Sasso Fetore." The citizenry will conclude this ritual by scrubbing the piazza after the execution.

"Barbarian conqueror," "throat of the past," "ancient tongue," "those before them," and "slings of barbarians" are allusions made during Hawkes's judgment supper to a racial heritage. That the present cannot transcend the past is clear. The men have adopted "the brown shirt and the wide-brimmed black hat" which covered "the first inhabitants"—a "primitive monastic order"—and the subservience and savagery which characterized "creatures who chanted while fighting on the early slopes of Sasso Fetore, pair by pair beating each other with hard fists under the watch of Superiors."

The Eucharist does not represent the only ritual perverted through a death-oriented heritage in *The Owl*. That novel's action, like *The Cannibal*, takes place during Pentecost or the Christian festival commemorating the descent of the Holy Ghost upon the apostles on the day of the Jewish harvest festival. This is ironic because the land remains infertile and the single virile male or prisoner will be crucified, flayed, and hanged. His executioner reminds the totemic owl of their blasphemous covenant: *"Thus stands the cause between us, we are entered into covenant for this work, we have drawn our own articles and have professed to enterprise upon these actions and these ends, and we have besought favor, and we have bestowed blessing."*

More prevalent in Hawkes's work than either Eucharistic or Pentecostal rites, the once sacred dance undergoes perversion too. At the fair, where "in the past some were got with fornication and games, in the time when there were men," a youth dances a gavotte with a dog while "young girls watched covetously." Regarding such dogs, the narrator explains:

This whole breed had once been deprived and whipped, tied ascetically by the lay brothers on the slopes. The bitches were destroyed. And the rest, heavy of organ and never altered with the knife, day after day were beaten during the brothers' prayers, commanded to be pure unmercifully. The dogs tasted of blood given in mean measure but were not permitted the lather, the howl, the reckless male-letting of their species.

These dogs symbolize the sexually deprived people associated with such contranatural myths and rituals.

Hawkes's awareness as a mythmaker fluctuates. His parodies in *The Beetle Leg* and *The Lime Twig* required considerable knowledge of the western and the thriller and his father-daughter pattern in *Second Skin* some knowledge of the Trojan War and *The Tempest*. But, at times, he is uncertain about myth and legend. One interviewer records him as saying, "Now, I'm not so sure on 'Artemis' and I'm not really good on classical areas but am I wrong or is Artemis the Greek version or the Roman version of Diana?" [20] Understandably, then, Hawkes "wasn't that aware" of *The Lime Twig*'s Christian symbolism and was ignorant of *The Beetle Leg*'s Osiris myth (Interview).

Conscious or unconscious, his manipulation of myths shows them to have many functions. Sometimes they signify landscape-setting, as when the swamp on the Floating Island (*Second Skin*), the subtropical area surrounding the motel (*The Innocent Party*), and the deluged land near Mistletoe (*The Beetle Leg*) suggest paradise lost through Edenic imagery. Sometimes they convey tone, as when *The Beetle Leg* parodies the western and *The Lime Twig* parodies the thriller, and sometimes they delineate character, as when Cassandra becomes identified with the Blessed Virgin Mary (*Second Skin*), Larry with Satan (*The Lime Twig*), and Adeppi with Christ (*The Goose on the Grave*).

Such allusions also operate at the structural and thematic levels. Michael's swinish behavior is dramatized in *The Lime Twig*'s Circe episode, and his rise and fall in its Icarus symbolism. In *Second Skin* and *The Beetle Leg*, mythology simultaneously provides landscape-setting, tone, characterization, action, and meaning.

External and human nature grow more ambivalent for Hawkes after 1960 and so do his myths and rituals. In *The Lime Twig*, where the countryside appears indifferent rather than hostile, Michael performs an act of atonement in the guise of Christ, though Larry, in the guise of Satan, survives him. And, in *Second Skin*, where the paradisiacal Floating Island holds an ominous swamp, Skipper represents both Eros and Thanatos.

This novel, epitomizing post-1960 ambivalence, concludes with a chapter entitled "The Golden Fleas." In addi-

tion to the myth of the Golden Fleece, it involves the ritual
of Halloween. On All Saints' Eve, Skipper escorts Sonny,
Catalina Kate, and her newborn child to the cemetery.
They choose a grave, light candles, consume bread, sausage, and wine amid singing birds and laughing celebrants.
The author's contention that the scene depicts continuing
life is justified by evidence from *The Golden Bough*. Frazer
says Halloween, "which marks the transition from autumn
to winter" was "the time of year when the souls of the
departed were supposed to revisit their old homes," and "in
modern times . . . has been attended by picturesque features and merry pastimes, which rendered it the gayest
night of all the year." More significant is the claim that the
ancient Celts probably dated "the beginning of the year
from [Halloween] rather than from Beltane [May
Day]," [21] Figuratively, then, Catalina Kate's infant enters
the world on New Year's Eve.

Also according to Frazer, however, Halloween produces witches as well as departed souls, superstition as well
as celebration, death as well as life, an ambivalence *Second
Skin* reveals when Skipper observes, "It was hard to know
whether all those shades were celebrants honoring the dead
or the dead themselves preparing a little fete for Kate's new
child." Later, he asks her, "Who do you think it looks
like . . . Sonny or me?" and she answers, "Him look like
the fella in the grave."

The Golden Fleece myth recurs during the Floating
Island sections of *Second Skin*. Both Skipper and Jason
travel across water to another land, searching for a hide
symbolizing potency. Jason sows dragon teeth with the help
of two fire-breathing bulls and Skipper inseminates cows
with the help of Oscar, "the bull in the bottle," who be-
grudges "every invisible drop." Whereas the fleece and
Medea become Jason's prizes, Skipper remains impotent.

This impotence, made clear at the cemetery through ambiguity over the paternity of the baby, is rendered comical
at the "grove of perpetuation." There three women and two
men watch as four heifers—Phyllis, Alma, Beatrice,
Gloria—and two steers—Edward, Freddy—perform. The
animals "think it is time for a hot fete," so Alma, Beatrice,
and Gloria attempt "to mount each other or one of the two
steers" and Freddy uses "his nose for life." When Edward
jumps Phyllis, Skipper declares: "And my namesake
—reluctantly I admit that name—left bright thick gouts of
mud on each of Sweet Phyllis's soft flanks." Then Skipper-
Edward inseminates this fertile cow with a "long amorous
pipette" containing a "few pure drops of Oscar."

These later myths and rituals, like Hawkes's later settings, convey an attitude toward interrelated human nature
and external nature which altered between *The Goose on
the Grave* and *The Lime Twig*. Whereas his pre-1960 myths
and rituals are negative in a world controlled by Thanatos,
his post-1960 myths and rituals are ambivalent in a world
challenged by Eros. He moves from the static, death-
oriented position of the early work to the dynamic position
Freud outlined in *Civilization and Its Discontents*:

The natural instinct of aggressiveness in man, the hostility of each
one against all and of all against each one, opposes this pro-
gramme of civilization. This instinct of aggression is the deriva-
tive and main representative of the death instinct we have found
alongside Eros, sharing his rule over the earth. And now, it seems
to me, the meaning of the evolution of culture is no longer a
riddle to us. It must present to us the struggle between Eros and
Death, between the instincts of life and the instincts of destruction, as it works itself out in the human species. This struggle is
what all life essentially consists of and so the evolution of civilization may be simply described as the struggle of the human species
for existence.[22]

Freud's thesis anticipates Hawkes's post-1960 world, a world where people manifest natural aggression, where aggression comes from and represents the death instinct, where instincts of destruction struggle against instincts of life, and where the struggle is for existence. Even when Hawkes seems most hopeful, Michael perishes as Eros, and when most affirmative, Skipper survives as Thanatos. Not until *The Blood Oranges*, which dichotomizes Life and Death, do unambiguous life-affirming myths and rituals appear.

Though Hawkes embraces Freud's instinctual thesis, he also subscribes to the progressive deterioration view of history recorded by Eliade. Originally, myths like the Fisher King–Osiris and rituals like the Eucharist–Fish-Meal endorsed life, but at some unspecified point during the past barbarians took over (*The Owl* and *The Blood Oranges*). Their descendants have debased those old paradigms; and because these descendants have created only vulgar substitutes, Hawkes satirizes them through the comic modes of parody, burlesque, and travesty.

Not all ancient myths and rituals were positive, since antique as well as modern man was victimized by the same aberrations. Hawkes's view of one, incest, suggests that his position on these is psychological rather than religious. To him, incest signifies harmful repression, not dangerous expression. Incest and other desires inhibited through taboo result in artificial controls that he abhors, such as religion and law, and in irrational behavior, such as violence and war. When man imposes analogous restraints on creatures and forces outside himself, failure ensues. Thus, coercing the dogs in *The Owl* entails their extermination, and damming up the river in *The Beetle Leg* brings human devastation. If there was a paradise to lose, it was not the biblical paradise of innocence and ignorance, but the Hawkesian paradise of free love and enlightenment.

# 3

# My Time of No Time

Hawkes started writing poetry during high school and the early years of college. The Harvard University Printing Office privately published his volume *Fiasco Hall* (1943) and *The Harvard Advocate* his poems "Little Beatrice" and "The Magic House of Christopher Smart" (1947). The 1947 pieces are more sophisticated than the 1943 pieces, but no one poem is distinguished. Most treat the romantic theme of unrequited love and use end rhyme and archaic diction. That Hawkes first wrote poems is nonetheless important because it helps to explain why he turned to *lyrical* prose. When he stopped composing poetry and began writing fiction in the late forties, he retained poetic impulses and methods, as the fiction also drew upon psychic or unconscious materials.

Hawkes, the poet, became a myth-maker who speaks about mythical or repetitive time:

The contemporary part of [*The Cannibal*] is dated 1945 but that date is supposed to be taken as something to disregard. The time of that novel is simply in the future—remember it begins with all of Germany coming out of an insane asylum into a devastated landscape. And it ends with the success of the neo-Nazi movement which in turn results, positively and ironically, in the return of the whole country to an insane asylum. And this as you say, is posed against the literally historical period of 1914, the First World War. I suppose this juxtaposition at the outset is intended to try to suggest that perhaps we don't move so much in cycles as repetitions or that we have always had these particular problems of violence, destruction, sadism and so on.[23]

Repetitive time permeates the post- as well as the pre-1960 fiction. It is in Hawkes's favorite season, summer, that Cassandra's honeymoon, Tremlow's mutiny, and Skipper's father's suicide take place in *Second Skin*. Also preoccupied with the interval between twilight and dawn, he focuses on 2:00–6:00 A.M. in *The Lime Twig*. Thick beats Margaret and Sybilline seduces Michael during these nightmare hours; destiny for Hencher revolves around 3:00–4:00 A.M. when his mother died, his feelings over "home" grow acute, and his skull gets crushed; at 3:00 A.M. Annie visits Michael, and at about 4:00 A.M. Cowles killed the proctor.

Other kinds of repetition contribute to Hawkes's mythopoeic orientation. One that he consciously considers poetic is implied in his article "The Voice of Edwin Honig," [24] where he discusses Honig's "physiological imagery." "Nature and nature imagery are dominant" and "visions of houses are forever recurring" in the Honig poems to form image chains that provide unity, coherence, atmosphere, and meaning. Hawkes's critical sensitivity toward such chains stems from an artistic reliance on them. He uses iterative imagery, especially involving animals, deformity, clothing, external nature, military, and mechanical phenomena.

The use of color to render *Second Skin*'s landscapes and

characters is typical. Green and yellow recur during the fictional past as ominous. There green describes Skipper's tattoo, Miranda's kerchief, Fernandez's automobile, guitar, and socks, Cassandra's eyes and dress, the Kissin' Bandits' uniforms, the awning, tent, and turf involved in Gertrude's funeral. Miranda's slacks, Captain Red's oilskins, and Cassandra's burial place are yellow. During the fictional present, however, the connotations of the same colors are so ambivalent as to verge on inversion. The iguana of the Floating Island may be green, yet the several trees are too, and though the swamp contains "dark green tepid sludge" and "bright yellow turds," yellow and gold transmit the Life-Force. Skipper, who states, "Gold was my color," calls his son in "The Golden Fleas," "Good as gold."

Like green and yellow, black and white are ominous during the fictional past. For example, "The Brutal Act" chapter, which recounts Tremlow's mutiny, keeps before us the white lifeboat and the black pelican. These non-colors also characterize the Gentle Island sections, where the old clapboard house and the tower of Dog's Head lighthouse are white and nearly everything else black. Because Skipper associates Miranda with death, as he does chauffeurs and hearses, her countenance mirrors her black clothing. The mistress of "two fat black Labradors" and "bold black handwriting" has a mouth that resembles "a big black broken flower," "black eyes and sockets," "black tangled hair." Black—and white—become inverted during the fictional present, however, for then Skipper and Sonny parade around in their white clothing amid life-oriented black women. When Skipper, Sonny, Catalina Kate, and the "little black fuzzy baby" arrive at the cemetery, they celebrate by eating black blood sausage and drinking white wine.

White is used straightforwardly to picture the innocent

white man Skipper and the "white" black man Sonny. It is
used ironically to picture *Second Skin*'s disloyal white
women. Miranda has white clothing, white surroundings,
"a great black and white head," "broad white face," and
"enormous white throat." There is only one significant allusion of this kind to Gertrude, whose color seems to be pink.
Skipper wants her buried in "a white casket with just a touch
of silver." On the other hand, many white (and silver)
references are made to their daughter Cassandra, nowhere
more strikingly than during the honeymoon sequence. She
wears a crocheted white dress and white Indian shawl and
possesses diamond pendants, silver breasts, a white hand,
two silver bracelets, and a silver fertility charm. Later, Skipper stresses Cassandra's silvery aspect in relation to a white
plastic Madonna. This ironic comparison, the whiteness of
Fernandez, and the silveriness of Honeymoon Hide-Away
establish white, like black, as symbolic of sexual betrayal and
its concomitant death.

Metamorphic characterization is an important element
in such long twentieth-century American poems as *The
Waste Land,* where Eliot's protagonist metamorphoses
from the poet himself to the Fisher King to Ferdinand to
Tiresias to the poet to a girl to St. Augustine during "The
Fire Sermon" section. *The Lime Twig* also uses this technique, Hencher first reappearing as Cowles, then as the
constable. Two other figures merge identities during Chapter 6: Throughout the novel Margaret represents the
child-adult and Monica the adult-child. Having played adolescent games together, these mutually compassionate,
half-clad victims of adult physical and psychological sadism
occupy adjoining beds and share the same ginger cake after
Margaret's beating. The merging of their personalities begins with Margaret taking Monica's nightmares "to be her
own bad dreams, as if in soothing the child she could soothe

herself." Soon the sobs of each probably coincide, and "when Margaret sobbed aloud, Monica sat up screaming." This interpenetration finally climaxes: "Now Margaret's sobs and Monica's screams commenced together and continued together, variants of a single sound, screaming and weeping mingled. . . . So Margaret felt the two sounds coming from herself, starting from the same oppressive breast, as if the other half of sadness was quite naturally fear."

Metamorphosis or something similar occurs between works too. Several characters from "The Nearest Cemetery" appear in the Gentle Island portions of *Second Skin*.[25] Better defined and developed, Captain Red, Jomo, and Blud, who are unrelated in the story, become one family during the novel. No longer the barber-narrator's brother-in-law or the Princess's lover, Blud turns up there as the boy Bub. Captain Red remains the bald-headed, middle-aged master of the *Peter Poor*, while Jomo, boasting a newly acquired artificial hand, is still wearing a baseball cap and has "black hair plastered down with pine sap." Captain Red's mother displaces Jomo's, and Skipper's mother becomes Mildred, the name of the barber's wife.

Among the recurrent figures, the Princess has greater significance than any except the narrator, for she inspired the three principal *Second Skin* females. Like Miranda ("princess, poor princess"), "The Nearest Cemetery" Princess wears slacks; like Cassandra, she is a young mother; and, like Gertrude, an unhappy wife. Skipper, evolving from the barber-narrator and from Hencher, becomes Edward in *The Undertaker*, where his morbid father again appears, and Cyril in *The Blood Oranges*.

Some repetitive techniques are not necessarily poetic—Hawkes's recurrent actions and circular endings, for instance. When he said *The Cannibal* "begins with all of

Germany coming out of an insane asylum. . . . And it ends . . . in the return of the whole country to an insane asylum," he drew attention to a future recurrence that concludes several novels. Cap Leech, who missed Mulge, will push "one town further" during *The Beetle Leg;* the police, who unsuccessfully investigated Larry's gang, will unsuccessfully investigate Hencher's death during *The Lime Twig;* and Skipper, who supervised a daughter and grand-daughter in the Gentle Island portions of *Second Skin*, goes on to supervise a surrogate-daughter and grandson in the Floating Island portions.

Mythical time treats the eternal patterns of human behavior and so is indefinite as well as repetitive. Asked to tell what day and year it was, Balamir of *The Cannibal* replies, "*Weiss nicht.*" Later, Zizendorf says, "What was the hour? No one could know because there were no clocks." Just as Hawkes expresses the repetitive aspect of mythical time through iterative imagery and metamorphic charac-terization, he expresses the indefinite aspect through two other techniques identified with modern poetry and the cinema: associational flow and spatial juxtaposition.

*The Waste Land* contains many instances of associa-tional flow. In "The Fire Sermon" section, after the young man carbuncular deserts the typist, she "puts a record on the gramophone" that leads to the music Ferdinand hears that leads to "The pleasant whining of a mandoline." There is non-temporal coherence in Hawkes's "The Nearest Cemetery" too. Time is indefinite except for vague refer-ences like "next Saturday." Both the story and *Second Skin* employ first-person narration, but whereas the novel is a dramatic monologue with interspersed dialogue, the story more nearly resembles an interior monologue. The barber, totally unaware of his audience, narrates associatively. He remembers the sights, sounds, and smells the day the marshal drove him from Bloody Clam Shell Island to prison. Passing Jomo City, he observed Jomo's mother; recollecting her now he calls up the Princess, a presence he will feel again when the old woman appears wearing the dead girl's perfume. Even at the outset the prison struck the barber as another island, just as it strikes him now as another lighthouse where each man—Captain Red, Jomo, Blud—has a mental Venus. The barber cut their hair here, once having injured his finger remembering Jomo and the Princess. Such thoughts give rise to a series of associations: the Princess's loquaciousness, the ear, the seductive things she said, Mildred at the organ, self-impressions.

"The Fire Sermon" also makes use of spatial juxtaposition as Eliot's protean protagonist visits the Thames, the dull canal, London (the typist's room, the Strand, Queen Victoria Street, Lower Thames Street), the Thames (Greenwich, the Isle of Dogs, Richmond, Margate Sands), and Carthage.

Sharon Spencer has discussed the implications of spatial juxtaposition for twentieth-century fiction:

When events in time are spatially organized according to the techniques of juxtaposition that are employed in montage, they lose both their inevitable, sequential nature and their quality of irreversibility. . . . At its simplest, the spatialization of time in the novel is the process of splintering the events that, in a traditional novel, would appear in a narrative sequence and of rearranging them so that past, present, and future actions are presented in reversed, or combined, patterns; when this is done, the events of the novel have been "spatialized," for the factor that constitutes their orientation to reality is the place *where* they occur. One of the most obvious effects to be achieved by means of this process is simultaneity: the representation of two or more actions in different places occurring at the same moment in time. In this way, a novelist may activate a great many characters in a great many situations that are intended to take place simultaneously, or he may dissolve the distinctions between past, present, and future as they are dissolved in dreams and in the stream-of-consciousness flow.[26]

Hawkes's architectonic novels sometimes display a rearrangement of events which organizes past, present, and future in reversed, or combined patterns and which helps make the place *where* they occur their basic connection with reality. Although the years move backward, then forward during *The Cannibal* (1945–1914–1945), the seasons move forward, defying chronology by progressing from April (fictional present) through summer, fall, and winter (fictional past) to April (fictional present). This arrangement depends on the juxtaposition of Spitzen-on-the-Dein and das Grab, and it follows a prologue dealing with the "actual" present (fictional future). Whereas *The Cannibal* achieves simultaneity by alternating five separate tangential plots, *The Lime Twig* does so by alternating Margaret's beating at the Roost with Michael's orgy at the widow's parlor. Chapter 6 announces "It was 4 A.M.," then works backward to Thick's symbolic rape and forward to Larry's real rape; Chapter 7 announces "It was 2 A.M.," then reports Michael's sexual exploits and concern for Monica. Six begins later than 7, but the beating and the orgy are two actions in different places taking place at the same moment in time.

*Second Skin* demonstrates Hawkes's tendency to synchronize time and space. It begins and ends on the Floating Island (fictional present), which, except for sections two, three, eight, and nine, he alternates with another major setting, the Gentle Island (fictional past). In "The Nearest Cemetery," Bloody Clam Shell Island and the prison are counterpointed solely to contrast the barber's past and present, but in *Second Skin* the juxtaposition of Floating Island and Gentle Island has more meaning. Here Hawkes manipulates geography symbolically, the Gentle Island being a northern setting, New England, and the Floating Island a southern one, the West Indies. Skipper's apparent escape from death-oriented Western society to the primitive, Edenic, life-oriented Floating Island is paralleled by his previous odyssey across North America, the epitomization of civilized decadence. His odyssey originated on the West Coast and terminated on the East, carrying him ever deeper into occidental darkness. He believes he has abandoned the tempest of reality (Gentle Island) for the tranquillity of unreality (Floating Island). "Unlocated in space," the latter seems "quite invisible . . . a mirage" which Skipper describes with the words "romance," "pageant," "pastoral." That he also believes he has escaped time is indicated by the recurrent phrase, "my time of no time," and the final words, "The sun in the evening. The moon at dawn. The still voice."

Repetitive time, metamorphic characterization, and iterative imagery, which produce recurrence, and associational flow and spatial juxtaposition, which create indefiniteness, function in both Hawkes's pre- and post-1960 fiction to establish a mythopoeic vision of reality. The pre-1960 novels, written soon after Hawkes abandoned poetry, rely almost exclusively on these mythopoeic modes of organization. They therefore resemble long modern poems like *The Waste Land.* Such poems are circular, not linear, moving around a center that remains fixed and that involves all men in all places at all times. Such poems are synecdochical because each part, regardless of how small it may be, expresses the whole. Compared to the increasingly dramatic novels, the pre-1960 ones seem inert, static rather than kinetic, imagistic rather than dynamic. Lacking a clear-cut protagonist and controlling plot, their form may be termed "decentralized." *The Beetle Leg* and *The Cannibal* vividly illustrate this.

Mythical Mulge functions like Faulkner's Candace Compson, Addie Bundren, and Thomas Sutpen insofar as he represents a "cubist object." He is peripheral, however, to the sketchy controlling plot or to the main present action which includes the events leading to the climactic attack on the Red Devils. These events seem dissociated from that climax, since the attack grows out of the Red Devils' recurrent entrances—at the ranch, at the jail, at the dormitory, at the Metal and Lumber Gymnasium, at Old Lifeline—and not out of the posse's behavior. Wade and the Sheriff have been preoccupied with Leech, and he, in turn, with his profession, while Bohn has been concerned with the Finn and Luke with Camper. Such distractions do not prefigure the attack, an event which becomes inevitable only after Leech gasses the Sheriff and the seven men join forces. Yet three subsequent scenes—at the bottleneck, at the red wagon, at the dormitory—interrupt the narrative flow, and, when the controlling plot resumes, four instead of the original seven men are still together. *The Beetle Leg* achieves structural coherence, but does so through a motif rather than sequentially arranged incidents. This motif—the search—affects all the characters, whose personal quests are mirrored in the communal quest for Mulge. The resulting frustration *unconsciously* inspires the pursuit and ambush of the Red Devils.

Ma, the pioneer woman, and Lou, the sophisticated outsider, undertake parallel odysseys during *The Beetle Leg* that reinforce its search motif and that operate as tangential plots or self-contained actions unfolding simultaneously with the controlling plot. Ma's personal quest directly embodies the communal quest. Leaving her ranch, she finds the divining rod, then wanders from bluff to dam, calling, "Oh, Mulge. Where are you, Mulge?" Two chapters later she is last glimpsed high above the bottleneck, still seeking, still summoning. The tangential plot that involves Lou is not so ritualistic or direct, yet it too reinforces the central motif of the communal quest. In Chapters 1 and 3 the Campers try to find a town he dimly remembers; in Chapter 3 they reach a familiar dormitory, Camper goes fishing, and Lou encounters several people, one of whom she queries about Camper's amorous past; in Chapter 4, during a card game, she hears the question, "Oh, Lou, Lou, where is he at now?"; and in Chapter 6 she asks the welders the same thing, but their responses confuse Camper with Mulge, the ordinary mortal become a myth who has deserted them.

Up to this point, Lou's odyssey resembles Ma's: both are abandoned females pursuing faithless males. In Chapter 10, however, Lou extends the meaning, if not the action, beyond the controlling plot. Forsaking his own futile search, Camper rejoins his young wife at the dormitory, and while he fumbles over a useless pistol, she leans against the window through which a voyeuristic Red Devil had stared. There she fantasizes about being detained by a deputy who takes Camper for a pimp and her for a prostitute. When she looks again, she and the Red Devil merge and she whispers, "Take me out of here." Lou, the only character in *The Beetle Leg* to acquire self-awareness, has acknowledged universal evil and exorcised the search-object. Perhaps she will escape.

Her experience is rare in Hawkes's fiction, for his tangential plots ordinarily clarify rather than extend meaning, as is demonstrated in the five contiguous actions of *The Cannibal* treating Stella-Balamir, Stella's crippled son, the Mayor, Herr Stintz-Selvaggia, and the Duke-Jutta's boy.

Had the last action not been introduced, the title would be obscure, since the Duke's "fox hunt," which ends with Stella accepting her second floor boarder's breakfast invitation, is the single instance of actual cannibalism in the novel. Its dual significance—devouring one's own kind and betraying one's own young—is supported by two other tangential plots and counterpointed by a third.

Stella's crippled son changes from unwitting victim to unwitting victimizer. Discovering the Duke and Jutta's boy downstairs at the theater, he inadvertently helps the Duke capture the boy; later, in a sexual revery, he thinks, "The boy certainly deserved the cane." In the other supportive plot, Herr Stintz, the tuba-playing schoolteacher, practices despotism among children and duplicity among adults. His abduction of Jutta's daughter to force her to witness Leevey's assassination is in character. Stella's kindness toward Balamir, the madman she nourishes and protects, forms an ironic contrast to these supportive plots but it too helps clarify meaning.

Without such actions, the climactic event would be misleading because Leevey's death, while symbolizing the genocide the Nazis directed against the Jews, involves a German and an American rather than compatriots. Without them, Hawkes's central idea of devouring one's own kind and betraying one's own young would be abortive or obscure even though Zizendorf's gestures are "cannibalistic": he deceives an imprisoned friend, taking over his newspaper and his wife; he murders two men also implicated in a countryman's execution; and he decides that Jutta's offspring must depart once National Headquarters is established. The conclusion focuses on the adult victimization of children. When Zizendorf commands Selvaggia to "Draw those blinds and go back to sleep," "She did as she was told."

A device related to the tangential plot, the analogous action or corresponding event, is also prevalent in the pre-1960 novels. Whereas tangential plots are interrupted stories characterized by beginnings, middles, and ends, analogous actions are isolated occurrences producing suggestive clusters. Both reflect meaning rather than advance movement.

*The Cannibal* and *The Beetle Leg* have several analogous actions. During *The Cannibal,* Leevey's murder climaxes a series of assassinations, commencing with the death of the Archduke Ferdinand, then Pastor Miller, and, finally, Herr Stintz and the Mayor. Promiscuous sexual relationships abound too—Zizendorf and Jutta, Leevey and the slut, Herr Snow and Gerta—as do voyeurism and vigilance—the Census-Taker watching Zizendorf and Jutta copulate, Zizendorf and his followers awaiting Leevey, Herr Stintz ogling Selvaggia, Selvaggia peering out her window. These "unconscious" patterns of parallel activity provide structural cohesion and thematic insight. They present the whole book through its various parts; they show how murder, lust, and impotence are constant, general.

One crucial instance of analogous action from *The Beetle Leg* has been mentioned: those efforts made by the Sheriff, Cap Leech, and Luke to eradicate noxious growth. Related is another pattern emphasizing compulsive talking. In the prologue and Chapter 2, the Sheriff "stopped reading, marked his place, and began to talk"; in Chapter 8, medicine man drugs law man with talking gas; and in the epilogue, the first declares, "Now I'll talk." A Third *Beetle Leg* pattern—cruelty toward animals—pervades Hawkes's fiction. Here the Red Devils injure a pointer, Bohn slays a cow, and Leech a rooster. Like children, such creatures are victims.

Had sectional titles and numbers not been used extensively in the pre-1960 novels, their decentralized form would be harder to follow. Only *Charivari* introduces topical and numerical ordering concurrently—Courtship (1–6), The Bachelors (7–9), The Wedding (10–11), Rhythm (12–15)—to give it simultaneous linear and episodic structuring and to indicate the logic beneath what would otherwise be a labyrinthian accumulation of events.

Hawkes's subsequent pre-1960 novels title and number sections sequentially. *The Goose on the Grave* is illustrative: 1, 2, Edouard, Interview with the Alpini, 3, 4, Adeppi's Dream, 5, The Confession, 6, 7, 8, Palms, 9. Although still difficult, the controlling plot has become less so because of captions designating chapters that wholly or partially interrupt story line or shift the narrative focus. The controlling plot records the successive involvements of Adeppi with adults: Nino and Edouard, Jacopo and Gregario, Arsella and Pipistrello, Brother Bolo and Dolce. These lead to the boy's ultimate flight, just as adult oppression leads to *Charivari*'s climax, the reconciliation of Emily and Henry.

The sequence of titled and numbered sections is most elaborate in *The Cannibal*, whose form uniquely depends on parts. Part One—1945 contains two chapters, One and Two; Part Two—1914 contains four, Love, Stella, Ernst, Lust; and Part Three—1945 four more, Tonight, Leader, Land, Three. The headings are useful because they indicate that World War I, which divides World War II, represents the past which the present emerged from but also another instant of time reflecting the timeless human situation; that the past as a single unit, assimilated by the author if not by the characters, exhibits a coherence the present lacks; and that the third part of the novel concludes the first ad fulfills the second, anticipated when Ernst passes the line of statues: *"love, Stella, Ernst, lust, tonight, leader, land."*

Hawkes has said, *"The Owl* was written in the first-person as an effort to rewrite *The Cannibal"* (Interview). This remark is interesting because the later novel represents his initial attempt at dramatic structuring. Unlike the decentralized *Cannibal* (1949), *The Owl* (1954), focusing on the fictional present and containing little exposition and no flashbacks, treats similar material without the need for tangential action. Sectional headings disclose only a controlling plot whose beginning, middle, and end are clear: The Prisoner Comes, The Synod and the Sentence, The Prisoner Escapes, He Hangs.

Although more bewildering to the reader, the earlier *Cannibal* has a controlling plot, which suggests that even Hawkes's decentralized fiction never totally abandons narrative movement. In Part One, Zizendorf and the Census-Taker go from the newspaper office to Stella's boarding-house, where Zizendorf and Jutta make love before venturing forth to join the dancers at the low clapboard storehouse. When Jutta escorts the Census-Taker home later, Zizendorf unites with his followers along an embankment. In Part Three, they are still awaiting Leevey, who eventually shows up, is killed, robbed, and buried. Returning to the newspaper office, Zizendorf sends his followers to Command Two, Stella's chicken coop, and, afterward, informs Jutta about the night's activities and murders one eyewitness, Herr Stintz. Soon he reunites with his followers at the chicken coop to clean it up and print an "Indictment" that will restore German autonomy. The followers distribute this while the future dictator and Secretary of State cremate Herr Stintz and the Mayor.

Tangential plots and analogous actions reinforce the

central meaning in controlling plots throughout the pre-1960 novels, and sectional headings provide their direction. Consequently, the incidents of *Charivari* (courtship-marriage), *The Cannibal* (devouring one's own kind and betraying one's own young), and *The Goose on the Grave* (child-adult involvements), though decentralized, become sequences leading toward and away from climactic events as surely as the prisoner's experience during the more dramatic *Owl* begins with his arrival and ends with his execution and its aftermath.

Climactic events—abortion (*Charivari*), assassination (*The Cannibal*), massacre (*The Beetle Leg*), hanging (*The Owl*)—are nearly all violent. They often involve purgation. On the one hand, society to resume its status quo exorcises an alien force embodied by a person or persons: Germany expels the Allied overseer, Clare and Mistletoe a band of lawless invaders, Sasso Fetore a foreign soldier. On the other hand, the individual disburdens himself of some sort of external or internal pressure: Emily of an unwanted baby, Adeppi of Urbino's crazy grown-ups. Such purges are ironic, for society's status quo turns out to be depraved and the individual's new-found freedom illusory.

Though the pre-1960 fiction is not wholly without controlling plots and climactic events, its form, except in the dramatically structured *Owl*, is anti-dramatic. Controlling plots are disjunctive, so that they must be reconstructed through sectional headings and interpreted through tangential plots and analogous actions. Moreover, decentralized characterization accompanies decentralized structure, eliminating the traditional protagonist and diffusing the reader's attention among various figures. With structure and characterization de-emphasized, everything relates to the meaning at the core as in *The Waste Land*. Constant circling about a pivotal concept produces static rather than kinetic, imagistic rather than dynamic art. This is the art of the poem, not the play.

Hawkes has written plays as well as poems. A Ford Foundation fellowship enabled him to study for a year (1964–65) with The Actor's Workshop of San Francisco, where he completed *The Innocent Party*, prefaced by Herbert Blau, a co-founder of the company, who said, "The very tedium of the worst rehearsals struck [Hawkes] as the thing itself. He responded to the collective feel of the form. He came as an observer and became a participant, the director's alter ego." [27]

Like his mid-forties poems, Hawkes's mid-sixties plays are undistinguished in themselves, but just as the poems help to explain the mythopoeic structure of the pre-1960 novels, the plays help to explain the dramatic structure of the post-1960 ones. Having written and published the San Francisco pieces when he did was no accident, for Hawkes's momentary involvement with the theatre and playwriting coincided with his discovery of the conflict between Eros and Thanatos. He has termed the resulting shift from decentralized to dramatic form as being a shift from "pure vision" to "the conventional novel": "Of course it's obvious that from *The Cannibal* to *Second Skin* I've moved from nearly pure vision to a kind of work that appears to resemble much more closely the conventional novel. In a sense there was no other direction to take." [28] This evolution, which began in *The Lime Twig* with the discovery of the conflict between Eros and Thanatos, has continued in *Second Skin* and *The Blood Oranges*.

The third person *Lime Twig*, like the first person *Owl*, contains basically only one plot, the controlling plot. It is rendered by a split narrative focus involving Michael and Margaret Banks. In Chapters 1 and 2 his life away from the flat (Artemis, quay, van, Highland Green) alternates with hers at the flat; in Chapters 2–8 his life outside the Roost (public lavatory, Pavilion, Baths, Spumoni's, widow's parlor, paddock) alternates with hers inside the Roost. Save for the temporal transposition of Chapters 6 and 7, the Bankses' joint journey toward death advances chronologically. Michael abandons Margaret to pursue brutal, erotic dreams. He follows Hencher, finds Rock Castle and Larry's gang, experiences Hencher's death, encounters three "back-luck fellows," meets Sybilline, witnesses Cowles's murder, seduces lascivious women, challenges the constable, and stops Rock Castle; meanwhile Margaret, who misses him but nevertheless enjoys her own sexual hallucinations, leaves the flat to pursue Michael, joins Little Dora and Larry via the train, suffers confinement, attempts escape, gets beaten and raped, cries out and is hustled off. Margaret's adventures, no less than Michael's, form part of the controlling plot because they too constitute the fictional present. His conflict over Eros (Love-Life) and Thanatos (Death-Lust) arises from the guilt he feels whenever he contemplates or sees her. That guilt, together with the analogous action of Chapter 7 (fighting the constable after the constable shoots Monica), prepares for the climactic event of sacrificial atonement as Michael frustrates the horse and hence the gang.

*Second Skin* has a controlling plot treating the fictional present and a vertical plot or flashbacks treating the fictional past. Their organization suggests that these plots parallel one another. Like *The Lime Twig*'s split narrative, both move forward chronologically. Incidents in the controlling plot are ordered according to the stages of Catalina Kate's pregnancy (Eros)—at Plantation House, at the swamp, at the grove of perpetuation—and culminate on Halloween when she, Skipper, and Sonny celebrate the birth of their son (climax). Incidents in the verticle plot chart Cassandra's deterioration (Thanatos)—at the Chinatown café, at the tattooer's, at the cheap eastern hotel, at Miranda's—and culminate with her suicide, ostensibly over an illegitimate fetus (climax). The inextricable relation between the two plots is further established by the fact that the fictional present is the period during which Skipper recreates the fictional past. The first chapter ends, "on to the high lights of my naked history," and the last, "this final flourish of my own hands."

Hawkes's only post-1960 novel employing sectional headings is *Second Skin*. Chapters in the fictional present—Naming Names, The Artificial Inseminator, Vile in the Sunshine Crawling, Land of Spices, and The Golden Fleas—are juxtaposed to chapters in the fictional past —Agony of the Sailor, Soldiers in the Dark, The Gentle Island, Cleopatra's Car, Wax in the Lilies, The Brutal Act, and Drag Race on the Beach. Besides expressing the substance, continuity, and interdependence of controlling and vertical plots, these headings show how *Second Skin*'s past (seven chapters) outbalances its present (five chapters) even though the book begins and ends during the present.

Another orienting device used more often before 1960, the prologue, is later increasingly integrated. *The Cannibal* prologue divulges almost nothing about narrator, setting, or action. Spoken after the fact, the two paragraphs comprising this section merely assert that for three years Zizendorf has led Spitzen-on-the-Dein, that his tenure was broken with exile in a foreign land where he composed *The Cannibal*, and that he will return. *The Beetle Leg* prologue, published two years later, is much fuller. Called "The Sheriff," in its eight and one half pages there is developed a believable narrator whose remarks introduce the novel. Through the tale of the little girls as told by the Sheriff,

Mulge already has mythical proportions. Here, action, setting, and theme are anticipated. Concerning the fictional past, the prologue tells how the Sheriff first saw Mulge, how he speculated that the river would entangle him, and how he attended Mulge's marriage to Ma; concerning the fictional present, it reveals that Luke's "record is still clear." The Sheriff focuses on fourteen years of human lawlessness and natural treachery. What he was reading prior to speaking sums up the waste land motif: *"Seed planted when the Earth is in Leo, which is a Barren, Fiery Sign, will die, as it is favorable only to the destruction of noxious growth. Trim no trees or vines when the Moon or Earth is in Leo. For they will surely die."*

The prologue to the post-1960 *Lime Twig* is Hawkes's best piece of short fiction, partly because the narrator has greater complexity than any other Hawkesian personage except Skipper. Hencher links World War II (fictional past) and its aftermath (fictional present). According to him, he met Larry, a dishonorably discharged captain, and Sparrow, a crippled ex-corporal, during the war. Even then Larry as air raid warden was characterized by kindness, often inquiring about Hencher's mother, while Sparrow as dope addict was characterized by loyalty, always obeying Larry's commands. Juxtaposed to this distant fictional past is the immediate fictional past when the narrator became involved with the Bankses. These children of the war were born victims. Sympathetic, Michael, as Hencher's tolerant new landlord, welcomed him back, and Margaret, his innocent new landlady, called him "affectionate." Hencher, who wanted a "home," gradually took over, directing their lives, enjoying their possessions. And, gradually, his narrative moves from the immediate fictional past toward the fictional present—"I still fix them breakfast now and again"—in which he perishes while luring Michael and Margaret into Larry's trap. Besides preparing for subsequent actions and characters, through elaborate exposition, *The Lime Twig* prologue also establishes place: Hencher lived at Highland Green (prologue), where he dies (novel), and his mother died at Corking Street, where he lives (prologue). Once Lily Eastchip's, Corking Street has been refurbished—"electric buzzer," "three flats," "spirit shop," "deck chairs" (prologue)—improvements prefiguring the changes to be wrought by the gang (novel). This twenty-five-page overture obviously achieves a high degree of integration with what follows.

Hawkes employs orienting devices like sectional headings and prologues less frequently after 1960, but when he does, as in *The Lime Twig* and *Second Skin*, they have a closer connection to the books they serve than they did to the decentralized fiction published before 1960. Their growing assimilability accompanies the shift from "pure vision" to "the conventional novel," a shift made clear by the chronological actions governing the post-1960 work. Although Hawkes during 1964 claimed his novels were not elaborately plotted, these actions conform to the traditional definition of plot: "A planned series of interrelated actions progressing, because of the interplay of one force upon another, through a struggle of opposing forces to a climax and a *dénouement*." [29] Struggle, climax, dénouement —all dramatic words—aptly define fiction portraying the conflict between Eros and Thanatos.

If the reader, accepting Hawkes's tacit challenge to participate in the creative process, reorganized the events of the pre-1960 novels along chronological lines, they would form cause and effect patterns that would show the past dominating the present. This means a discoverable continuity lay beneath such books as *The Cannibal*, a continuity anchored in deterministic thinking, since 1914 inevitably leads to 1945 and has molded people like Stella, Jutta, and Ernst through racial, historical and biographical factors.

Yet Hawkes's early, decentralized fiction, which moves around pivotal concepts, emphasizes mythical or repetitive time, whereas his later, sequential fiction develops conflicts among forces and emphasizes historical or chronological time. And, because the linear movement of the latter is better suited to the presentation of cause and effect, as well as conflict, the post-1960 books are more obviously deterministic, as well as more dramatic than the pre-1960 books. Determinism—the doctrine that neither external nor human choices are uncaused, but result from antecedent conditions, physical or psychological—unmistakably constitutes the philosophical basis of *The Lime Twig* and *Second Skin.*

*The Lime Twig* prologue (fictional past) determines *The Lime Twig* action (fictional present):

On the thriller level, Hencher is literally a member of Larry's underworld gang, is an instrument of Michael's fatality. . . . But of course you're right that Hencher's introduction serves as a prologue to all the episides of the novel in which Michael's fantasies become real. Michael and Margaret Banks were conceived as representing England's anonymous post-war youth . . . while I saw post-war England itself as the spiritless, degraded landscape of the modern world, in this case dominated by the destructive fatality of the gambling syndicate. But it seemed to me that the drab reality of contemporary England was a direct product of the war, and that Michael and Margaret were in a sense the innocent spawn of the war. However, since Michael and Margaret were mere children during the war, incapable even of recalling the bombing of London, the problem became one of dramatizing the past, of relating wartime England to post-war England, of providing a kind of historical consciousness for characters who had none of their own. Hencher served this function. He became the carrier of Michael and Margaret's past as well as of their future; I thought of him as the seedbed of their pathetic lives.[30]

Elsewhere called "the purveyor of the seeds of war" who brought "the war forward into the adult lives of Michael and Margaret," [31] Hencher stands for violence and death.

"Naming Names," the first chapter of *Second Skin*, functions like *The Lime Twig* prologue to establish tone, place, character, and background, as if the novel were a play. Several matters are treated in the chapter, but it is dominated by Skipper's self-vindication, which occupies the long opening, and his disastrous childhood, which occupies the even longer close. In Skipper, Hawkes juxtaposes illusory freedom and actual bondage, rationalized innocence and unwitting guilt. The exposition introduces an all-powerful past, and flashbacks—Cassandra's honeymoon, Gertrude's funeral, Tremlow's mutiny, Fernandez's murder, Papa's suicide—sustain it. Skipper himself accentuates temporal sequence by calling his "serpentine tale" a "diary," a "chronicle," a "history."

Since the fictional past has shaped the fictional present, *Second Skin* opposes the sunlit now and the moonlit then until the concluding chapter where the Night of All Saints and the Floating Island join. Both time schemes entail an elaborate chronology enabling Skipper to project backward and forward freely. Catalina Kate's pregnancy progresses in the fictional present: in chapter four, she is three months pregnant; in seven, six; in ten, eight; and in twelve, the girl gives birth at the very hour of the day that Skipper, now fifty-nine, decided on in chapter four.

Two areas make up his fictional past. The first, leading up to and including the Gentle Island portions, which end seven years before the fictional present, is ordered by a symbolic rendering of the seasons totally absent from "The Nearest Cemetery." The high school dance occurs during the Christmas season; the *Peter Poor* incident in March; the drag race and Cassandra's suicide in May; Skipper's departure in June. In these portions, winter and spring mean sterility and death; whereas on the Floating Island, spring, summer, and fall are the seasons of fruitfulness and life.

The second area, the "far-distant past," uses summer ironically, for summer is the season of Cassandra's honeymoon, Tremlow's mutiny, and Skipper's father's suicide. Those events have also been carefully dated. Cassandra's marriage precedes Pixie's birth by seven and a half months and Gertrude's suicide (Christmastime) by sixteen. The father's suicide happened when Skipper was "small and fat and ungainly"; Tremlow's rebellion when Skipper was serving aboard the U.S.S. *Starfish*. During World War II, Gertrude slept with his crew and sent him V-letters. Fernandez's murder, described in a "far-distant past" section, actually took place on Skipper's final shore patrol, just prior to his arrival at the Gentle Island, where, two or three months later, he notified Cassandra. Following a tight temporal sequence, this "far-distant past" shapes the past as certainly as the past does the present.

Fictional present, past, and "far-distant past" may *appear* simultaneous from the spatial juxtapositions of memory, yet such distinctions are not dissolved in *Second Skin*, for the narrator's dramatic monologue—unlike dreams and stream-of-consciousness flow—is a self-conscious, highly organized explanation to the reader or unseen auditor-judge. Even when Skipper feels he has discovered timelessness through placelessness, Hawkes undercuts him by making the paradisiacal Floating Island mortal. Evil persists there: the life-giving water wheel does

not work; the religious Sister Josie is a "thin devoted example of missionary madness"; the innocent Sonny has an
"incurable case of boils"; and the fertile Catalina Kate must
suffer an iguana on her back. Perversely attracted to decay
and death, this adolescent black female not only dozes in
the swamp, where she wishes to bear her child, but, in
another ominous setting, the cemetery, she answers the
question about whom the baby resembles with the remark,
"Him look like the fella in the grave." Thus, the curve of the
fictional present action (the birth of a son) which parallels
the curve of the fictional past action (the death of a daughter) is ironic: the son's mortality is emphasized immediately
after his birth.

Hawkes never spatializes time to the point where it
constitutes a fourth dimension, as Eliot attempts to do in
his *Four Quartets*. Events do not lose "their inevitable, sequential nature and their quality of irreversibility" even
when he inverts chronological order. For example, though
the time in Chapter 7 of *The Lime Twig* begins earlier than
the time in Chapter 6, cause and effect nonetheless prevail.
Robert Scholes has commented on this:

Margaret suffers because of Michael's involvement with the people who make her suffer. Not only does she become hostage and
victim so that the gang will have maximum control over Michael,
but, specifically, some of what she suffers has been directly and
immediately caused by Michael's actions of the same night
—actions which are presented to us *after* we see their results so
that we apprehend them colored by their consequences. We are
forced to see them ethically.[32]

Scholes explains how Larry, who bruises Sybilline's eye
during Chapter 7, slashes and rapes Margaret during

Chapter 6 as a revenge for the way Sybilline and Michael have behaved.

Hawkes's evolution toward the conventional novel, where plot involves struggle, climax, and denouement, occurred because he abandoned a death-oriented, non-conflictive, decentralized world for a life- and death-oriented, conflictive, dramatic world, but not because he abandoned mythical time for chronological time. His fiction, which combines poetic and dramatic methods, has two purposes: to show that neither external events nor human choices are uncaused and to indicate "that we have always had these particular problems of violence, destruction, sadism and so on." Sequence and repetition become, therefore, correlation rather than antithesis. As a result, *Second Skin* is both romance, pageant, pastoral and diary, chronicle, history. It is, indeed, a "time of no time."

# 4

# Figures in the Carpet

During the mid-sixties, the words "hope" and "affirmative" entered Hawkes's vocabulary. About *The Lime Twig* he said, "This ending along with the novel's general pairing off of sensual and destructive experiences to me suggests a kind of hope. The fictional rhythm itself is in a way hopeful," [33] and about *Second Skin*, Skipper "undergoes all kinds of tribulations and violations and by the end of the novel, I think we do have, in effect, a survivor. This is the first time, I think, in my fiction that there is something affirmative." [34]

The feelings of hopefulness over *The Lime Twig* and affirmation over *Second Skin* spring from an authorial assumption that Michael and Skipper as psychologically complex protagonists *choose* Eros. Neither dupe nor pawn, Michael destroys the golden bowl and so foils the gangsters' plans and atones for his wife's betrayal; ineffectual Skipper struggles against his daughter's suicide and, perhaps, fathers his mistress's child.

Hopefulness and affirmation were soon compromised, however, when Hawkes admitted, right after *The Lime Twig* statement, "I'm reluctant to argue too strongly for the necessity of hope." [35] In the B.B.C. broadcast he later expressed both pleasure and perturbation that American readers and reviewers, who had previously associated him with "nightmare . . . the grotesque, the deformed, the decomposed," found *Second Skin* "uplifting." His uneasiness increased because an inmate of San Quentin, comparing the novel adversely to the earlier work, said it "was becoming affirmative in the wrong way, was somehow becoming weaker, too close to what we ordinarily think of as human or affirmative." Answering this charge in the same B.B.C. broadcast, Hawkes called *Second Skin* "a comic novel," "pastoral not merely in creating an ideal or idyllic vision of life," but in exposing "the barbs . . . hidden beneath the flowers." Then he recounted the death of Skipper's father lest others adopt the inmate's view.[36]

Hawkes's uneasiness is understandable, since, despite the new conflict between Eros and Thanatos, the post-1960 like the pre-1960 novels are essentially deterministic and thus negative. During the pre-1960 novels, mythico-historical and familio-environmental phenomena shape the behavior of the people inhabiting Spitzen-on-the-Dein and das Grab, Mistletoe and Clare, Sasso Fetore and Urbino. These cause-and-effect patterns continue to govern events in the post-1960 *Lime Twig*. There Hencher's death only "appears accidental": "He is killed because he didn't obey orders. Also because finally as a henchman he got too close to the victim, Michael Banks. And Larry the Limousine wants that victim for his own." [37] Earlier, Hawkes had explained: "Like Michael Banks, Hencher —because of his need for love—is killed by the race horse; if we understand Michael's own story then we understand Hencher's death." [38]

Neither *The Lime Twig* nor *Second Skin* provides charac-

ters with a mythico-historical background of barbaric ancestors to shape present behavior as do *The Cannibal, The
Owl, The Goose on the Grave,* and *The Blood Oranges,* but
familio-environmental forces make both deterministic.
That Michael and Margaret in *The Lime Twig* lack natural
parents is of no great significance, since Hencher, himself
victimized by his mother, becomes their surrogate parent,
serving and ensnaring them. Margaret's double, fatherless
Monica, lives with a promiscuous mother amongst gangsters. Though she recalls even less about World War II than
the Bankses, the war literally touches Monica when Sparrow seizes her arm where "under his fingers was a vaccination still bandaged." This ex-corporal, possessing silver
knee caps and a tattoo, is as much "the purveyor of the seeds
of war" as Hencher, a war whose past violence Larry keeps
vividly alive. Having "been the first to carry [Sparrow]
the night he screamed" and having "later drowned the
operator of the half-track," the ex-captain now walks in
footsteps "like those of an officer on parade," hums "some
sort of regimental march perhaps," and plays "a barracks
song."

   Comparable familio-environmental forces affect *Second Skin.* During his childhood, Skipper experiences his
father's suicide and his mother's abandonment, and, during his adulthood, his wife's infidelity and his subordinate's
mutiny. Yet, like *The Lime Twig* victims, he suffers most
after "the wave of wrath was past."

   Paradoxically, as Hawkes's characters become freer,
their lives become more fated. Symbolized by German destiny in *The Cannibal* and divining rod/zodiac in *The Beetle
Leg,* fate grows into a strong force in *The Lime Twig* and
*Second Skin.* Michael knows "that Margaret's hand has
nothing in the palm but a short life span" and that "what-

ever was to come his way would come . . . slowly out of a
thick fog." Later, he remembers an "ugly voice" which asks,
"Why are you always reading obituaries? . . . Who do you
expect to find on the lists?" Prognostications, the reiterated
phrase *"Feeling lucky?"* the poster *"You Can Win If You Want
To,"* the sign *"Win with Wally,"* show fortune omnipresent in
*The Lime Twig*'s public world, while dreams reveal its private
world of desire. Slyter receives a communication from
Bailey—"My poor lame sister dreamt it now three nights in
a row, that the horse will win"—which suggests that these
public and private worlds are interconnected. Public hap-
penings dramatize private wishes: when Michael stops "his
own worst dream, and best . . . the flesh of all violent
dreams," he stops the race too.

Like Michael, Skipper often refers to fate. The "sad
little prophetic passage from my schoolboy's copybook"
foretells "this particular journey" that "I always knew myself destined for." He has sensitive skin and his "true subject
may prove to be simply the wind." He has a tendency
toward seasickness and mistrusts the nautical life. Both
fickle, air and sea stand for chance and chance helplessness—helplessness Skipper counters with superstition.
He considers the pelican a good sign during the *Starfish*
episode, but on the *Peter Poor* the gulls bring a morning
curse.

The psychobiological bases of Hawkes's determinism
are manifested directly through mythico-historical and
familio-environmental forces and indirectly through uncontrollable external nature or unpredictable cosmic nature: the earth *mirrors* human noxiousness and lawlessless
(*The Beetle Leg*, *The Innocent Party*) and the universe human
capriciousness and apprehensiveness (*The Lime Twig*, *Second Skin*). It could be argued that for Hawkes human,

external, and cosmic nature form a single essentially
malevolent phenomenon.

He has made several explicit remarks concerning
human nature. In "Flannery O'Connor's Devil," he con-
gratulated her and Nathanael West on "demolishing man's
image of himself as a rational creature." [39] The phrase,
"tangled seepage of our earliest recollections and origina-
tions," appeared in another 1962 article, "Notes on the
Wild Goose Chase." Having also mentioned "that nightly
inner schism between the rational and the absurd" and "the
terrifying similarity between the unconscious desires of the
solitary man and the disruptive needs of the visible world,"
Hawkes admitted: "I myself believe very much in the sack
of the past slung around our necks, in all the recurrent
ancestral fears and abortive births we find in dreams as well
as literature." [40]

Dreamlike moments frequently occur during
Hawkes's work and confirm his preoccupation with the
unconscious and the irrational. Of three *Charivari* sequences involving the Expositor, only the first two are
called dreams. This reflects a general tonal shift from fantasy to surrealism, in which the author eases the reader
from outside a nightmare situation to inside it. Dream one
shows Henry anxious that Emily should bear a child and
become unfaithful. In dream two Emily, nine years old, is
attending a beloved grandmother's funeral and hears a
voice say. *"We are mourned only by children."* In dream three
the Expositor tells Henry his plight is the result of "a dream
of your omnipotence," then leaves him to mumble, "Look
out for dreams. Beware."

In *The Cannibal* the Mayor betrays guilt over the executed Pastor Miller in a recurrent dream; and in *The Owl*
the hangman envisions Sasso Fetore's destruction in a
dream "of the universe of the tribunal." Neither adopts the

dream technique as often as *The Goose on the Grave,* where
there are three dreamers and one daydreamer. Dolce
dreams about Edouard and a companion urging Adeppi
"to wail melodiously and beg" before the Vatican City gates.
Adeppi dreams about fatherless, wounded Nino in search
of somebody. And the novel closes with Nino's own vague,
though warm and continuous, dream. Meanwhile,
Edouard has had two daydreams. During the first, "He
found himself early in the century . . . in an Emperor's
garden" coming to know the "all-curried and handsomely
saddled world of pleasure"; during the second, he sees the
least fit surviving "the Sforza family . . . [which is] all but
dead" and "the Grand Hotel . . . burning."

Dreams also permeate Hawkes's post-1960 works. The
dramas are typical. A daughter dreams and pantomimes in
*The Innocent Party;* a son dreams about his father whisking
away his mother in *The Undertaker;* in *The Questions* a Young
Girl recounts her mother's version of her father's dream
about her mother, with "nothing else on top except the
bra," talking to some men and her mother's assertion she
would never "lose herself in dreams, like Papa."

The dream of Rock Castle is not Michael's sole fantasy
in *The Lime Twig.* Sybilline reminds him of "the women he
had thought of coming out of comfort stations," her legs
those "he had seen bare in the undergarment ads," and
Annie "was a girl he had seen through windows in several
dreams unremembered." At the public lavatory, three
eunuchs form "the triangle of his dreams"; at the widow's
parlor his orgy has dreamlike qualities. Nor do the nightmares of Monica and the hallucinations of Margaret, whose
"own worst dream was one day to find him gone," exhaust
this irrational world. Hencher functions as dreamer—
"a man must take possession of a place if it is to be a
home for the waiting out of dreams"—and dream-

detector—"Behind each silent face was the dream." He plays the nursemaid, Mary Poppins, to the Banks couple, who are husband and wife rather than siblings. In both the fairy tale and the novel, surrogate-mothers appear suddenly at English addresses ready to make infantile wishes come true.

Skipper of *Second Skin* dreams about more than his literary descendant, Edward, of *The Undertaker*. Besides the recurrent hallucination they share regarding their mother, he has nightmares over the past and reveries about the present and future. The Floating Island and the repetition of words like "dream," "fantasy," and "vision" heighten the unreality that self-avowed dreamer Skipper reinforces through several remarks bearing on the fate motif. "A few of us," he says, "are destined to live out our fantasies, to live out even the sadistic fantasies of friends, children and possessive lovers"; "history is a dream already dreamt and destroyed"; "still I felt that I knew the place and had seen that bicycle in my own dreams."

Whereas the pre-1960 dreams involve anxiety and wish-fulfillment, the post-1960 dreams, which might or might not come true, are prophetic. Determined by their psychic states, though paradoxically freer, characters begin to *experience* their fantasies—hence Michael's orgy, Margaret's rape, Skipper's flight. Such consummations reflect "the painful absurdity of sexual desire," Hawkes's definition of Nathanael West's dream.[41]

Post-1960 dreams also vary technically from pre-1960 dreams. The three Expositor sequences in *Charivari* show that even during the early books they have a structural purpose. But the orgy in *The Lime Twig* and the Floating Island in *Second Skin* employ the dream for more than simple recurrence. The controlling action of one dramatizes Michael's central fantasy, and the other

Skipper's vision. Thus, post-1960 works sometimes literally
*become* dreams.

Irrational human nature is evidenced by sexual aberrations as well as by dreams. These pervade the Hawkes
canon, where there are numerous examples of adultery,
sexual ambivalence, homosexuality, impotence, incest,
masturbation, nympholepsy, prostitution, rape, sadism,
sterility, frustration, and voyeurism. In *The Lime Twig*,
Michael and Margaret commit adultery, he physically, she
mentally. His sexual reveries, which result from impotence,
and hers, which result from virginal frustration, lead to
parallel beatings and rapes. When Michael thinks over the
orgy and confesses "he should like to try it, try some of that,
with Margaret," they are no longer the brother and sister of
*Mary Poppins*, innocent siblings enjoying a magical world.
The unconscious fear of incest lay behind Michael's impotence and Margaret's frustration in a novel where two sisters share the same lover and one son has an Oedipus
complex. Other aberrations emerge: Thick, who has "beat
girls before" and who aims "randomly at [Margaret's] ab-
domen and loins" while wearing only an undervest and
unbuttoned trousers, is a sadistic, impotent voyeur. Larry
shows latent homosexuality or sexual ambivalence when he
picks up Sparrow "carefully and coolly as a woman of long
service." Sexual ambivalence also marks Hencher with his
effeminate red-circled eyes and Little Dora with her masculine hairy upper lip. The three women who seduce
Michael at the boardinghouse brothel illustrate the recurrent theme of female promiscuity: "Or it was what they had
done in the shelters or when the bands were marching
—upright"; "It meant women going it upright beneath the
bridges."

As Margaret hallucinates about the partly clad sta-
bleboy, she hears mortuary bells outside. This implies an

association of sex with violence and death which characterizes the world that *The Lime Twig* people inhabit. At the
Men's, Michael recalls seeing "a man die on a toilet—from
fear," and, terrified, he soon sits on a broken toilet himself.
First, however, three eunuchs appear, one with an obscene
hatband. They reiterate, "*Sybilline's in the Pavillion*," warn
against escape, brandish pellet bombs. Later, Michael visits
another hell at the Baths, "a lower world of turning and
crawling and groaning men." This also has homosexual
overtones: "On either side of the door was painted the
greater-than-life-size figure of a naked man, one view seen
from the front, the other from the rear." Here a small boy
periodically throws ice water "across the flesh of a prostrate
bather and the man would scream." And here Michael is
indignant and the constable indifferent when three fully
clothed gangsters murder a nude fourth.

The victimization of the young by the old vividly expresses the irrational nature of humankind. In Hawkes's
fiction, adults often dominate children. During *Charivari*
Emily endures an overpowering mother, the generaless,
who "adjusted the knotted cord that tied Emily's feet"; and
Henry has an overpowering father, the parson, who ap-
plied the water torture while Henry's arms were "strapped
securely to his side." *The Cannibal*, where Ernst's father
"used" him "as a scapegoat to vent an angry desire for
perfection," where the Mother Superior "never could
. . . whip these girls into shape," concludes with a child
doing what "she was told."

Adults neglect as well as dominate children. If they are
not orphaned or abandoned, they are ignored. Neglect is
symbolized by isolated bands of children. In *The Cannibal*,
"they chased each other about the lobby and bowed when
approached by adults"; in *The Beetle Leg*, "they run
loose . . . like their parents"; and in "The Traveler," they

"ate no breakfast but went directly from their beds to the beach." The lack of communication between children and adults is typical of both the pre- and post-1960 work: "To him some rifleboy with a sack of powder at the hip," the old General in *The Cannibal* calls his daughter Stella "Stool." In *The Innocent Party,* another daughter lists her parents' "don'ts" and "won'ts"—dancing, listening, looking, reading, traveling, swimming, breathing—then screeches at her aunt, "They're trying to shrink my bosom! They don't want me to have a bosom!"

There is physical cruelty to children. *The Cannibal's* schoolteacher "drove the boys in the rain and made the girls repeat and repeat their lessons in the old schoolroom," and *The Beetle Leg's* doctor, who boasts he may "mark . . . children," damaged a boy by delivering him from a deceased mother with "wailing forceps."

There is mental cruelty too. In *The Undertaker,* the son remembers how the father spoke thirty years ago about "the seeds of death," "those dead Negroes," his wife's bloody demise, and the son's obesity. He then realizes: "All this time you've been the rusty fishhook lodged inside my brain." Mental cruelty becomes even more apparent when adults expose "innocent" children to evil. Selvaggia must watch adultery, perversion, assassination, and fire during *The Cannibal.* Adeppi witnesses abduction, betrayal, homosexuality, promiscuity, violence, fanaticism, simony, prostitution, brutality, and murder during *The Goose on the Grave.* Herself an involuntary observer, the Young Girl of *The Questions* decides, "It's not much fun to play in a world where everybody cheats."

War, the evil adult game that cuts across Hawkes's fiction, affects every child in *The Cannibal;* "Many boys had been crushed"; "Several girls were recently orphaned." Nor does distance insure immunity. Cassandra of *Second Skin* says, "My life has been a long blind date with sad unfortunate boys in uniform," and her infant endures "dreary abandoned days in wartime transit."

*The Lime Twig*, which encompasses nearly every aspect of the adult-child relation, frequently counterpoints "innocent" youth and "evil" age. For instance, on the train between Dreary Station and Aldington, Margaret talks with Little Dora, whose "body . . . clothing . . . hatpins and hair—all were greased with the smells of age." Little Dora asks her about her children, thinking they might be "parked out," and Margaret replies that she has none. Then Little Dora explains: "I was parked out more than I was home. For me there was nothing at the window, I used to eat my hands in the corner." Now, however, the aging gun moll with "a female warden's eyes" is "at the good end," since she often takes charge of a sister's kids.

During their conversation, Margaret feels that "each tie crushed under the wheels became a child." This allusion represents one of many to anonymous victimized children in *The Lime Twig*. Among others are the whipped boy Hencher remembers, the crying children Margaret hears, the sleeping boy Larry hits, the running child Michael imagines, the boys the Violet Lane detectives will beat. The book is full of specific victimized children and childlike adults who variously experience adult domination, neglect, mental and physical cruelty, war, and sexual perversion.

But though adult victimizers like Little Dora and Hencher were themselves victimized when they were children, they still subscribe to marriage and home. So does Sparrow. Drunk and surrounded by weapons, he directs Little Dora to "give us a hand with this present for my boy Arthur." Irony about domestic institutions continues as Larry promises her:

I'll make it up to you. I'll make it up for the twenty years. A bit of marriage, eh? And then a ship, trees with limes on the branches, niggers to pull us around the streets, the Americas—a proper cruise, plenty of time at the bar, no gunplay or nags. Perhaps a child or two, who knows?

Thus, a novel about marriage between ingenuous children ends with a marriage between corrupt adults.

In *Second Skin*, Cassandra illustrates the child's semi-conscious awareness of adult aggression and the result —arrested development. There are many references to her childishness: "baby fat and spangles and shoulder-length hair and dimples"; a green taffeta dress "for a fifteen-year-old. For a cute kitten." Among Hawkes's retarded characters, the most memorable are Henry and Emily in *Charivari* and Mauschel in "The Grandmother" and "The Traveler." Henry approaches his parents "a gaunt, cut-up, timid little boy." He writes to his fiancée, "Why don't they come and change my pants," fetches milk for his mother, and muses continually about his "dear Sister Ann." Another forty-year-old jackdaw, dwarfish Emily fears the dark, uses words like "daddy" and "mummy," dreams of childhood, and wears a baby cap, a blue jumper, and ribbons. She is "a tumble-stomach little doll" who has a kewpie doll, a toy chest, a book of paper dolls.

In "The Grandmother," Mauschel, ostensibly the son of Lebrecht and Metze (prostitute), makes faces, grins over his mother's illness, and dons black swimming trunks during dinner. Next day he winks at Uncle Justus Kümmerlich (miserable) through the kitchen window, one eye distorted; then this man-sized moron, whose fatness, wild hair, and wet shirt are emphasized, enters and puts an "arm like a dead reptile" around his mother's shoulders while placing what appears to be the banknote his uncle has given him on his mother's plate. But when she reaches for what turns out to be only a "piece of rubber counterfeit," Mauschel snaps it.

"The Grandmother" concludes with an enigmatic dialogue between Metze and her own dead mother which fails to explain the characters' attitudes. Those attitudes are clarified in a sequel, published later but dealing with earlier events. "The Traveler" contains an illuminating confession: Kümmerlich tells his wife, "You see . . . I am the father after all." The avowal is made during the purchase of the lamb eaten in "The Grandmother." This suggests incest as the cause of the intrafamily relationships and Mauschel's idiocy.

Mauschel is identified with the Jews through an abusive name meaning "sheeny." Other children are identified with Jesus, the archetypical Jewish sufferer: Ernst and the hotel children collect crosses in *The Cannibal*, and, "When [Stella] looked into [his] bed, she saw only a small black-haired Christ on the pillow." In *The Goose on the Grave*, Adeppi personifies Italy's sacrificial doves. Aside from animals, Indians, and Negroes, however, Hawkes rarely introduces victims pure and simple. Thus, a Jewish soldier helps execute a virtuous pastor, then consorts with a diseased whore before conspirators assassinate him (*The Cannibal*); a captured foreign prisoner on a brief reprieve senselessly slays four ganders (*The Owl*); and a motorcycle band terrorizes an entire region before it is ambushed (*The Beetle Leg*). Hawkes's children are no exception to this rule, for like the children who appear in *Les Chants de Maldoror* [42] by Lautréamont, a nineteenth-century French poet he greatly admires, they represent both victims and victimizers.

The fall from grace into paradise lost is the fall from

sexual expression into sexual repression, but Hawkes also sees human nature, and hence children, as *congenitally* corrupt. Adults and the adult world trigger that congenital corruption through aggressive behavior. Such behavior repeats itself; victimized by every adult he encounters, Adeppi of *The Goose on the Grave* directs a blind man toward a gruesome end. Fully aware of his violent dreams, his impurity, and his wife's short life, boyish Michael of *The Lime Twig* entangles, betrays, and abandons girlish but hardly innocent Margaret. Children grow up to affect other children, sometimes even their own offspring. In *Charivari,* a mother overpowers a daughter who then aborts her own baby; and, in *The Cannibal,* a father neglects two daughters who then ignore their own progeny.

Despite textual evidence to the contrary, Hawkes has consistently defended and justified his child characters. He asserted once, "almost everything I write relates in one way or another to the world of childhood and to innocence, for these are my two concerns, the making of a world, and the child. And in almost everything I've written the child usually dies." [43] Later he added, "children can be taken as authorial innocence, purity, and are the victims of our corrupt conventional, apparently moral but actually destructive world" and "my child characters are often destroyed if not corrupted" (Interview).

These remarks, which are optimistic in the sense that they emphasize childish innocence, echo Hawkes's feeling of hopefulness over *The Lime Twig* and affirmation over *Second Skin.* This optimism was tempered by uneasiness during the mid-sixties when he was "reluctant to argue too strongly for the necessity of hope" and pointed out "the barbs . . . hidden beneath the flowers." But by 1971 he argued, "It would be absurd to take my fiction as negative. It is quite the opposite" (Interview). Evil, formerly "one of the pure words I mean to preserve," [44] has now become merely "a powerful metaphor." Now Hawkes expresses no interest in the *sources* of Eros and Thanatos, though he believes that "they are culturally created" rather than innate. Nor does he "believe in any great satanic force existing outside of us or pursuing us from some dark past." Instead, "we ourselves do all the 'creating' " and "are each of us totally responsible for everything that is" (Interview).

Such statements reject determinism with its insistence upon cause and effect and its pessimistic bias. The act of choice between Eros and Thanatos which appeared after 1960 has since produced more and more positive triumphs: Michael over Larry, Skipper over Miranda, Cyril over Hugh (*The Blood Oranges*). Still, these triumphs remain *ostensible*. Not only is Eros less lucid and vivid than Thanatos, but every life victory terminates in extinction or impotence, so negative determinism continues to undermine affirmative free will. There are discrepancies, then, between what Hawkes thinks and feels, what he wants and gets, what he says and does, discrepancies which are reflected in the effect of his novels on the reader.

According to Hawkes, character, like those other "familiar ways of thinking about fiction"—plot, setting, theme—is one of "the true enemies of the novel." [45] By plot he means the usual definition involving struggle, climax, and denouement; when speaking of character, he accepts some conclusions Richard Chase reached in *The American Novel and Its Tradition:*

The novel renders reality closely and in comprehensive detail. It takes a group of people and sets them going about the business of life. We come to see these people in their real complexity of temperament and motive. They are in explicable relation to na-

ture, to each other, to their social class, to their own past. Character is more important than action and plot, and probably the
tragic or comic actions of the narrative will have the primary
purpose of enhancing our knowledge of and feeling for an important character, a group of characters, or a way of life.

Most of Hawkes's characters are not conspicuous for real
complexity of temperament and motive, explicable connections, transcendent importance. They are more nearly
characters from the romance, which, Chase contends, "can
flourish without providing much intricacy of relation," than
from realistic fiction. Figures from the romance,

probably rather two-dimensional types, will not be complexly
related to each other or to society or to the past. Human beings
will on the whole be shown in ideal relation—that is, they will
share emotions only after these have become abstract or symbolic.
To be sure, characters may become profoundly involved in some
way, as in Hawthorne or Melville, but it will be a deep and narrow,
an obsessive involvement. In American romances it will not matter much what class people come from, and where the novelist
would arouse our interest in a character by exploring his origin,
the romancer will probably do so by enveloping it in mystery.
Character itself becomes, then, somewhat abstract and ideal, so
much so in some romances that it seems to be merely a function
of plot.[46]

Hawkes, who has qualifiedly confessed to possessing "a
vestige of the romantic temperament" (Interview), nowhere resembles past romancers (and contemporary anti-
realists) more than in his treatment of character, since for
him too it "becomes . . . somewhat abstract and ideal, so
much so . . . that it seems to be merely a function of plot."
Subordinated with many other fictional elements making
up an overall design, most Hawkes people are typical instead of individual, often representing ideas or forces. This

he manages through several kinds of associations: names, roles, animals, objects, clothing, physical characteristics.

Some characters have mythical-classical names. *The Cannibal*'s Jutta and Balamir evoke a pagan Nordic past, and *The Lime Twig*'s Sybilline and *Second Skin*'s Cassandra are modern versions of legendary Greek figures. Rounding out the Agamemnon allusions in *Second Skin*, Skipper, who calls Miranda Venus and Cleopatra and Tremlow Triton, calls himself Iphigenia and Paris. In *The Innocent Party*, Jane "is an adolescent, part tomboy and part Aphrodite-as-young-girl," and as such approaches "a mythic force."

Historical-literary names, like the mythical-classical, become much more common after 1960, with the literary ones more common than the historical ones. Some Shakespearean names appear in *Second Skin*, where Skipper buries his unfaithful wife, Gertrude, and defeats his lustful arch-rival, Miranda. *The Tempest* supplies the most important Shakespearean names in *Second Skin* and in *The Innocent Party*. When Miranda conjures up Prospero's sweet, young daughter and Skipper claims to be "old Ariel in sneakers," the novel uses those names ironically. The play uses them directly. Phoebe describes her niece, who will enter "an awkward, girlish Caliban," as the "natural child" of Caliban and Ariel, for "she was both animal and angel."

Mythical-classical and historical-literary allusions constitute only one means for lending symbolic significance to people through their names. From *Charivari* on, other techniques are present, the most pervasive being the designation of people by roles rather than names or by names signifying roles. Hawkes adopts the dramatis personae device, as well as textual references, to connect people with roles. Its use in the story "The Nearest Cemetery" and in the play *The Innocent Party* illustrates his growing fondness for multitypical characterization or figures who represent more than one thing. After the location of "The Nearest Cemetery" is established—"a small state penitentiary in New England"—there follows a cast of characters playing various parts:

THE PRINCESS: summer visitor to Bloody Clam Shell Island; unhappy wife of a New York meat packer; woman of beauty; victim of the local barber.

MILDRED: the barber's wife.

CAPTAIN RED: lobsterman in his fiftieth year; first lover of the Princess.

BLUD: lighthouse keeper; Mildred's brother; second lover of the Princess.

JOMO: off-island gas station attendant and vicious small-town sport; third lover of the Princess.

THE BARBER: narrator; fourth and final lover of the Princess. He loved her from afar and killed her.

Though Beatrix is just "the mother" and Edward "the father" in *The Innocent Party*, Jane is "a mythic force" *and* "the daughter," and Phoebe is "Sportswoman, sophisticate, world traveler, heiress," *and* "the aunt." This dramatis personae device introduces the other plays too, but the characters in those plays perform only one role. In *The Wax Museum*, Bingo is "the young attendant," Sally Ann "the virgin," and Frank "her fiancé"; in *The Undertaker,* Father is "a small-town undertaker" and Edward "the undertaker's son"; and in *The Questions,* the Man and the Young Girl receive no further description.

In addition to the use of names and roles, Hawkes's people become ideas or forces by means of association with animals, objects, clothing, and physical characteristics. Frederick Busch considered animals so important that he wrote a master's thesis on the subject. Busch claimed that "the use of animals is, certainly, two-fold. On one hand, animals provide a kind of 'background music' for the mad virtuosity of solitary characters. . . . On the other hand, animals do more than serve thematic high points and a general atmosphere. They become characters, and characters become beasts." Busch found this double function running from *Charivari* through *Second Skin*, yet "the animal background music . . . tends to decrease as the human-animal, animal-human metaphor increases in concentration." *The Cannibal*, whose characters are less stereotypical than *Charivari*'s, supplies the first sustained animal metaphor, the fox hunt. *The Owl* pushes such metaphors to an extreme and manipulates animals "as almost allegorical figures instead of simply as reflectors of human qualities." People, however, dominate *The Lime Twig*. Consequently, they "are no longer described, move by move, word by word, *as* animals; their relationships and motivations, instead, are shown to be animalistic in subtle fashion through concentrated, underlying animal metaphor, not through an almost allegory-like insistence on a one-to-one ratio of human act to animal act." [47]

Although the human-animal pattern overshadows the animal-human pattern, elements of the latter appear during the pre-1960 work. For instance, in *The Cannibal* a monkey screams, "Dark is life, dark, dark is death," and in *The Goose on the Grave* a whelp howls, "Condittadino . . . Coraggio!" The cat, Mr. Cuddles, plays the collier's wife's familiar in *Charivari*. He enters wearing hat and tie, exchanges several lines of dialogue, mutters "give us a kiss" while asleep, then strolls across the room upright. Having acquired human characteristics, Mr. Cuddles has "lost his whiskers and part of his tail."

The human-animal pattern includes characters designated animals by name, behavior, and affiliation. The pos-

sible import of such identifications may be gathered
through two brief excerpts from Mr. Busch's thesis. Analyz-
ing *The Owl*, he comments: "It is appropriate that the prisoner, the owl's prey, becomes a bird himself. But the fleeing
bird also becomes predator. . . . The man fleeing from a
bird-murderer becomes, himself, a bird and murderer."
Later Busch discusses Skipper's tattoo: "It is this burden of
guilt, rendered reptilian skin—and, so capable of being
shed—that Skipper will exchange for his second skin." [48]

Although both objects and clothing characterize people, the latter is more important than the former. Jane, who
represents tomboy and Aphrodite, Caliban and Ariel,
wears a bikini throughout *The Innocent Party*. Her father's
"worn white linen suit" and her mother's "shabby blood-red
negligee" symbolize their poverty, and the mother's "out-
landish Victorian undergarment" their prudery. Costumes
reveal aunt Phoebe's wealth and carnality, for during the
first four scenes this masculine heiress sports bermuda
shorts, a black brassiere, a bright orange man's silk shirt,
and during the last three, a skin-tight silver lamé evening
gown. The action of many scenes revolves around clothing.
For example, Edward looks away when he finds Phoebe
partly covered, so she dons her shirt, which, however, remains unbuttoned; then, while Beatrix berates Phoebe
about poverty, Edward exposes his threadbare elbows and
ripped pants.

*The Wax Museum*'s action depends entirely on clothing.
It begins with the attendant, Bingo, lasciviously disarrang-
ing the uniform of George, a life-sized figure of a Royal
Canadian Mounted Policeman, and ends with the virgin,
Sally Ann, erotically tidying him up again. In the meantime,
by arousing Sally Ann through sexual advances and allusions, Bingo manages to exchange costumes. Flaunting the
virgin's silk stockings, jacket, and pocketbook, the atten-

dant will join the virgin's fiancé, an offstage voice but a real man, while the virgin, wearing the attendant's tunic, greets George, an onstage presence but a dummy. Promiscuous Bingo and chaste Sally Ann thus exchange roles as well as garments; yet, because both possess red brassieres, they are sisters under the skin.

Clothing makes several significant contributions to *The Undertaker*. It provides a contrast between the undertaker, who "wears a black suit with a flower in his lapel and a stickpin in his somber tie," and his son, who "wears a contemporary light-colored business suit with a white handkerchief . . . and a lurid tie." When the Father dresses in his deceased wife's "long-unused woman's negligee and enormous white garden hat," clothing is used to demonstrate his self-conceived role as his son's mother. In the son's dream, the Father wearing "a white driving cap and white driving coat, great eyeless goggles, and black muffler" symbolizes death.

Physical handicaps are yet another indication of the ideas and forces active in Hawkes's characters. These fall into recognizable patterns: mutilation, deformity, disease, and deterioration.

Mutilation usually results from military experiences in Hawkes's fiction, though the most memorable and full descriptions treat non-military situations. The two fox hunts—one early and figurative, one late and actual —illustrate this. When the Duke catches and kills Jutta's boy during *The Cannibal*, his efforts to dismember the body are minutely recounted: "He hacked and missed the joints, he made incisions and they were wrong as the point of the blade struck a button." The dismemberment of the fox during *The Questions* is no less detailed: "Your father and his rival wallowed in the greasy pit, stripping the white fat from the slender bones and cracking joints and squeezing small elastic viscous bulbs and yanking on cold tufts of fur."

Although these fox hunt butcheries reveal more about the butchers than the butchered, physical characteristics generally define both victims and victimizers. Luke, with tiny face and feet; Bohn, with "small lips, thin and stunted from a touch of the wailing forceps"; and the Finn, with "fluttering canes . . . braces grinding" in *The Beetle Leg*, are illustrations of deformity closely related to the mutilation pattern. Many figures display bodily defects having sexual implications. Hawkes's promiscuous females tend to be large-bosomed and masculine, his impotent males fat and feminine. One figure from *The Owl* vividly points up the connection between deformity and symbolic characterization:

Signor Barabo's heart, consciousness, and ambition ended in an appendage that housed the kidney and overhung his groin like a tapir's snout—blind sack he lightly rubbed while discoursing and guardedly measuring the passers-by. He had a large flap hanging from the shoulder under cover of his coat. On winter evenings when his old wife massaged it with liniment, he struck her and, enraged, leaned over again so that the deformity rose up with uncanny liveliness to be oiled. Outside he was a peasant, inside a fish whose concealed pouches could inflate to considerable size until he groaned in his own monstrous dimensions.

Many people in addition to those in *The Beetle Leg* have diseases. Their deterioration is often signaled by the state of their hair. Stella tries to disguise her baldness with "long, false, flaxen hair." Yet, neither baldness nor growing smaller or heavier can be averted, much less senility, which may strike even a young man. *The Beetle Leg*'s thirty-year-old

Bohn is nearly as decrepit as *The Cannibal*'s ninety-year-old
General.

Mutilation, deformity, disease, and deterioration do
not exhaust Hawkes's roster of physical characteristics. Certain others help define the various doubles in *The Lime Twig*,
for instance. Hawkes contrasts plain Margaret with sexy
Sybilline and Annie. All three girls are young and childlike,
but she possesses brown eyes, straight brown hair with a
single deep wave, anonymous knees and heavy calves, and
they big eyes, bright hair, and shapely legs. Monica,
Margaret's double during the action, also resembles her
mother and the widow's daughter. Although Little Dora's
special qualities—surly black eyes and facial hair—seem
remote from the widow's—soft buttocks and curls—both
the elderly and the youthful woman have in common
shortness, greasiness, and corpulence. *The Lime Twig* males
also share certain physical characteristics. As fat men,
Hencher is paired with Cowles; as small men, Sparrow is
paired with Jimmy Needles. The constable comes to be an
older version of powerful Larry, who is the physical opposite of emaciated Michael.

Physical traits, like roles, animals, objects, and clothing,
make Hawkes's people "rather two-dimensional
types . . . in ideal relation," who undergo obsessive involvements, and who, because of their abstract nature,
serve plot rather than characterization. Romantic figures,
they are well suited to allegorical writing: and *increased*
allegorization has accompanied the movement from decentralized to dramatic form.

The pre-1960 books did contain climactic events, but
such events scarcely resolved conflict—"the struggle which
grows out of the interplay of two opposing forces in a
plot." [49] Not using traditional plotting with its preconceived

incidents and logically related sequence, Hawkes had eliminated struggle and interplay. When form was decentralized, so too was character. Consequently, the early novels set groups rather than individuals against each other, groups that often seem ambivalent. For example, *The Beetle Leg* contains two opposing forces—the community and the intruders. Ostensibly, the community represents "good" and the intruders "evil," but only superficially since both are impotent and sadistic. Because in Hawkes's mind, all mankind suffers from the same psychic disorder, these forces exchange positions, victims becoming victimizers and victimizers victims, thus excluding conflict and resolution. The intruders intimidate the community, the community the intruders, but this occasions little interplay and less struggle. And, though *The Beetle Leg*'s decentralized action culminates with an allegorical battle, the winners as well as the losers are brutish.

Thanks to the shift toward dramatic form after 1960, the conflict between forces, while still ambivalent, becomes better focused. Allegorical wholes replace allegorical elements as individuals replace groups. The two contending forces in *The Lime Twig* are both figures and factions. As he does in the early novels, Hawkes dramatizes their conflict externally: Michael (St. Michael)–Christ vs. Larry–Satan. On this level Michael is manipulated during the first allegorical battle and killed during the second. But because Michael remains a human being, Hawkes may also internalize his conflict, giving the story additional suspense. Michael abandons Margaret (St. Margaret) to realize fantasies that promise erotic fulfillment. He boards an excursion boat ironically called *Artemis*, for his psychic journey will carry him away from Dianesque purity and, instead, toward impurity or Sybilline, the mistress of Larry. Michael's struggle between Innocence (wife) and Depravity (whore) commences as he encounters the novel's temptress and continues throughout their orgiastic interplay. It reaches a thematic climax when he attempts to save Monica (St. Monica) by challenging the constable and a dramatic climax when he attempts to save Margaret by challenging Rock Castle. Choosing Love over Lust, Michael dies with "a large rose . . . in his lapel."

"The Brutal Act" chapter of *Second Skin* represents another post-1960 allegorical whole. The two opposing forces are black-haired Tremlow, whom Skipper and his servant Sonny call "devil," and blond Mac, the Catholic chaplain. Mac has inspired Skipper to read the New Testament. Setting it aside at the outset, Skipper confronts mutinous Tremlow. Then Skipper and Mac, "a well-oiled team," perform Mass, Skipper assuming the role of Mac's acolyte as he helps him dress, takes out and puts away the cross, and wipes Mac's lips. This interplay, an allusion to boxing, and Sonny's exposition prepare the reader for a nocturnal battle. Youthful Tremlow, after intoxicating the crew with licentious dancing "so you couldn't tell whether he was a chief or one of them hula-hula girls," seizes control of the ship. He hits Skipper twice and they fall overboard "in a black embrace" to "the bottom of the white lifeboat." Their fight resumes there and the erotic imagery intensifies when the mutineers roll Skipper over a water cask and Tremlow rams his grass skirt against him. Now that "The Brutal Act" or Hawkes's central motif of sexual betrayal has been dramatized, God may intervene: "It was Mac. Mac with . . . vestments flying and . . . tiny face white with fear, Mac who flung down the rope end, hand over burning hand . . . pulled me back aboard. . . . 'Pull her up, Mac,' I whispered, 'for God's sake.' "

If several contemporary critics had not pointed out the mixed nature of allegorical figures, Hawkes's parallel gravi-

tation toward allegory and realistic/psychological characterization would be difficult to understand. In this connection, Robert Scholes has written:

In the great allegories, tension between the ideas illustrated by
the characters and the human qualities in their characterization
makes for a much richer and more powerful kind of meaning.
The great allegories are never entirely allegorical, just as the great
realistic novels are never entirely real. And, in allegory, it is often
the tension between the ideational side of a situation and the
human side which makes for the power and the meaning—and
the power *of* the meaning.[50]

Hawkes was obviously aware of this tension Scholes
cites when he discussed *The Lime Twig* during 1966. After
calling *Artemis* an ironically named boat, Michael "a very
ordinary, very commonplace, youngish man," and Larry as
"a demonic god," Hawkes spoke about the climax:

[Michael] runs, in effect, in the posture of the crucifixion . . . . there is a dove that flies up from a branch. He
throws himself in front of the horse race . . . stopping the
dream, because the horse race is equated with dream desires. In
it, you remember the great cloud of black smoke goes up from the
race track, the dust. And you recall that the name of that race is
"The Golden Bowl." Now I didn't know where Henry James got
the title of his novel, I simply was not that familiar with the Bible
but I used that title nonetheless for the name of the race. And I
think that [it] is significant that Michael Banks is destroying the
golden bowl of earthly pleasure at the very last moment of his life.
You could say, conceivably, that the ending of that novel is redemptive. I am very leery, however, of saying that because I am not
really a religious writer. I'm made uneasy by these materials, but
the fact of the matter is, they got in there and I think they work. I
think they are fictionally true. And I suppose that despite of all

my interest in evil, all my belief in the terrifying existence of Satanism in the world, I guess by the end of that novel I somehow intuitively must have felt the human and artistic need to arrive at a resolution which would be somehow redemptive. I had to have tried to absolve this man of what he had done because he wasn't only a pawn. He wasn't only a dupe of a fatality that was English poverty and legalized gambling and ruthless criminal activity. He went into it. He followed the dream and the dream happened to be destructive. . . . Oddly enough, I thought I was doing something absolutely impossible, improbable, in that action. But a friend of mine gave me a newspaper clipping, not long ago, about the fact that in the 125th running of the Derby in England—in that race, just such an accident occurred. . . . I was very pleased that life does imitate fiction.[51]

A non-religious writer who uses words like "redemptive," "evil," "Satanism," and "absolve," Hawkes acknowledges allegorical tension in this quotation by juxtaposing abstract allusions—*Artemis*, "demonic god," "crucifixion," "dove," "golden bowl"—to an "ordinary" mortal who is neither "pawn" nor "dupe" and who is enacting "fiction" that "life" could very well imitate.

Both the ideational and human side appear in *The Lime Twig* and *Second Skin*, causing a tension that affects action as well as characterization. Not only are Michael and Skipper part ideal, part real, but so are their experiences. Consequently, these novels contain dual structures—the external or ideational versus the internal or human. In *The Lime Twig*, Michael wins internally, since his impulse toward Love conquers his impulse toward Lust, though he loses externally, his atonement failing to save Margaret or vanquish Larry. *Second Skin* reverses the pattern. While externally Skipper triumphs over Miranda and others, internally the impotent man cannot conquer "those little black seeds of death."

Internalized conflict reflects Hawkes's post-1960 affinity for psychological characterization. Despite "the true enemies" statement, *The Lime Twig* and *Second Skin* do treat people with "real complexity of temperament and motive," explicable connections, transcendent importance. This shift from "pure vision" to "the conventional novel," from symbolism to realism, from flat to round characters was accompanied by two developments. On the one hand, unitypical figures gradually receded before multitypical figures; and, on the other, an early tendency to enter peoples' minds, evident in *The Cannibal* with Stella, Jutta, and Ernst, accelerated.

Though non-narrators sometimes display realistic attributes and narrators never altogether lose romantic attributes, Hawkes's evolution toward "the human side" drew upon first-person narration more often than third-. But even his storytellers do not exercise the freedom of choice the reader might expect from their increasingly dramatic circumstances, for the post-1960 ethical world is as deterministic as the pre-1960 metaphysical world.

# 5

# Voices

Hawkes has never completely abandoned third-person narration, for it recurs from *Charivari* in 1949 to "The Universal Fears" in 1973. In his work, third-person narration almost always means multiple perspectives rather than an omniscient author or a central intelligence. *Charivari*, prefiguring *The Lime Twig*, alternates the narrative focus between a husband and wife, but it also offers several additional points of view. Although Adeppi dominates *The Goose on the Grave*, the reporting sometimes shifts: to Edouard and Jacopo in "Edouard," to Nino and Dolce in "Interview with the Alpini," to Dolce and Brother Bolo in "The Confession." Subordinate viewpoints introduced after 1960 are much more closely integrated with the essential experiences of the work. The Hencher-Slyter passages in *The Lime Twig* have greater dramatic relevance to Michael and Margaret Banks than the subordinate perspectives of *Charivari* and *The Goose on the Grave* have to the protagonists in those earlier novels.

First- and third-person fusion during *The Lime Twig*, where Hencher's prologue and epilogue frame eight chapters and Slyter's newspaper columns precede nine, typifies multiple perspective as Hawkes conceives it. *The Cannibal* Part 2 is written in the third person, while Part I and Part 3 are both first person; *The Beetle Leg* Chapters 1–10 in the third person fall between the Sheriff's prologue and Cap Leech's epilogue which are first person. The two voices intermingle in all the early novels except *Charivari*, entirely third person, and *The Owl*, entirely first person, then separate after *The Lime Twig* with first person becoming the dominant narrative mode. *Second Skin* and *The Blood Oranges* therefore do not have the simultaneous immediacy and distance, the identification and detachment, characterizing *The Cannibal*, *The Beetle Leg*, and *The Goose on the Grave*.

Hawkes's growing preference for first-person narration produced this separation of voices. He said during 1964:

As far as the first-person narrator goes, I've worked my way slowly toward that method by a series of semi-conscious impulses and sheer accidents. *The Cannibal* was written in the third person . . . I simply went through the manuscript and changed the pronouns from third to first person. . . . When I finished *The Beetle Leg* (a third-person novel), I added a prologue spoken in the first person by a rather foolish and sadistic sheriff, and this was my first effort to render an actual human voice. Similarly, Hencher's first-person prologue in *The Lime Twig* (also a third-person novel) was an afterthought, but his was a fully created voice that dramatized a character conceived in a certain depth. This prologue led me directly to *Second Skin* which, as you know, is narrated throughout in the first person by Skipper who, as I say, had his basis in Hencher.[52]

Apparently, then, an evolution occurred among first-person narrators from Zizendorf to the Sheriff to Hencher to Skipper. Reference to the Sheriff as an actual human voice and to Hencher as a fully created voice suggests that this evolution has been marked by progressively more complex characterization. Elsewhere Hawkes explains that Zizendorf was "merely mechanical" and the hangman "more a godlike voice than the articulated personality of a genuinely created character." Hencher, "the source of Skipper in *Second Skin* who is, in turn, the source of Cyril in *The Blood Oranges*," made first-person narration "real and possible." In conclusion: "These three figures, each of them large, fleshly men, develop from one enormous figure to the next . . . there is a kind of rarefying of their roles and of their rhetoric" (Interview).

In addition to more complex characterization, the first-person evolution has been accompanied by increased authorial involvement. Hawkes's mid-60's assertions continue to stress detachment for the writing of experimental fiction, yet, paradoxically, reveal an unprecedented subjective involvement with his narrators.

This is illustrated by Hawkes's attitudes toward Sidney Slyter and William Hencher. In 1964 he despised Slyter's "snake-like character embodied in the ugly sibilance of his name . . . his callow optimism, his lower middle class English ego, his tasteless rhetoric, his vaguely obscene excitement in the presence of violence" that make him "one of the most degrading and perversely appealing figures in the novel." On the other hand, "Hencher is a thoroughly sympathetic character, though some readers would probably consider him . . . to be merely crippled, perverse, distasteful." [53] Later Hawkes went on to say that Slyter was "the only character in my fiction that might approach a genuinely damned state" because he "is incapable of love,

incapable of sympathy, incapable of identifying with anyone" and therefore "exists purely as a kind of mechanism of
curiosity," whereas Hencher is "trying to love, trying to
become involved in sexual experience, even if it is only
onanistic or masturbatory" (Interview).

Hawkes's bias against Slyter and for Hencher reflects
his central moral position. Exploitative Slyter, without
human sensibility, represents a non-involved, non-erotic
Death-Force; deprived Hencher, with human sensibility,
embodies an involved, erotic Life-Force. *The Lime Twig*
juxtaposes their voices through contrapuntal organization,
Hencher's prologue coming between Slyter's columns,
which preface every section except the epilogue. To consider Hencher, the henchman, worse than Slyter, the
blighter, ignores the compassion invariably extended toward victims-turned-victimizers who realize that *survival* "is
the point." Though "fixated on his dead mother" and ex-
hibiting "all of the liabilities of life," childlike Hencher does
struggle to exist. It could be said of him what Hawkes says of
another "good diabolical figure": "The world's hostility
would be leveled against Larry. He's the kind of outcast
working or trying to live against the greatest odds. He's
exerting himself and his own loneliness to attempt to create
a world" (Interview).

Authorial identification with first-person narrators was
initiated by Zizendorf, Hawkes's earliest diabolical intelligence as storyteller:

. . . in revision I found myself (perversely or not) wishing to
project myself into the fiction and to become identified with its
most criminal and, in a conventional sense, least sympathetic
spokesman, the neo-Nazi leader of the hallucinated upris-
ing . . . the teller of those absurd and violent events. The
result was interesting, I think, not because *The Cannibal* became a
genuine example of first-person fiction, but because its "nar-

rator" naturally possessed an unusual omniscience, while the authorial consciousness was given specific definition, definition in terms of humor and "black" intelligence.[54]

Pleased when a student asked, "Do you think you are the Devil?" Hawkes contends such "satanic posturing" leads to "authorial-authoritarian detachment" which may be dramatized and sustained "through attacking sacred figures or sacred institutions." Because he regards psychic self-exploitation as impersonal, it never leads to purgation or expiation: "I cannot think of that inner life as mine. It is the inner lives of all of us, the inner chaos, the negative aspects of the personality" (Interview). Consequently, attachment versus detachment—an admitted paradox —causes him no disquietude.

His essay, "Flannery O'Connor's Devil," expands upon these convictions about the diabolical intelligence. According to Hawkes, the fiction of "moral" writers like Flannery O'Connor and Nathanael West frequently depends on immoral impulse. Fictive authority and immoral impulse are connected and the Devil's voice is the vehicle for satirizing, for envisioning "our godless actuality." He declares: "the diabolical attitude . . . lies behind the reversal of artistic sympathy . . . the 'meanness'-pleasure principle."[55] Years later Hawkes elucidated this, giving the reason he too identifies with satanic characters:

If the point is to discover true compassion, true sympathy, then clearly the task is to sympathize with what we ordinarily take to be the most repulsive in life, hence identification with the so-called criminal or rebellious mentality. I think of the act of writing as an act of rebellion because it is so single and it dares to presume to make the world. That's a kind of godlike act. I enjoy a sense of violation, a criminal resistance to safety, to the security provided

by laws or systems. I'm trying to find the essential human experience when we are unhinged or alienated from familiar, secure life
(Interview).

Wolfgang Kayser, also concerned about the diabolical
intelligence, calls the grotesque "an attempt to invoke and
subdue the demonic aspects of the world." [56] In a chapter
entitled "The Satanic Humorist as Narrator," he analyzes
Bonaventura's 1804 novel, *Nachtwachen* (*Night Watches*).
There "grotesque perspective" entails formal and conceptual elements resembling those the early Hawkes employs.
Kayser claims the novel "indulges in caricatural exaggeration," displays "profuse imagery . . . with its own laws of
association," and is "loosely structured . . . individual
episodes . . . strung together." "Meaningful things
. . . have no meaning," "familiar objects . . . look
strange," "the insane seem to be the most reasonable people."

Though both Hawkes and Bonaventura are satirists
who place their readers inside the book, they differ in their
conception of first-person narration. In *Nachtwachen* the
protagonist wears the satanic mask; in *The Cannibal*, the
author himself does. Furthermore, when pronouns were
converted from third to first person, Zizendorf of *The
Cannibal* was left describing phenomena only Hawkes could
know: for instance, most material in the third-person section that was filtered through Stella and Ernst and even
some material in the first-person sections. This reminds the
reader of *Les Chants de Maldoror*, where pronoun shifts
indicate a similar confusion over identification-
detachment. Like Bonaventura's night watchman, Maldoror wears the satanic mask; but unlike Bonaventura,
Lautréamont vacillates between "I" and "he," alternately
merging with, then separating from, his protagonist.

Hawkes claims that only his pre-1960 narrators are brutal and despotic: "I guess now that I don't necessarily make the connection between the first-person narrator and the sadistic mentality or the authoritarian stand . . . . the narrator of *The Owl* is a dictator, a fascist leader, but Hencher is not diabolical or satanic. Nor is Skipper, nor is Cyril" (Interview). Zizendorf, the Sheriff, and the hangman, however, by no means exhaust the sadistic mentality and the authoritarian stand, for vestiges of both appear after 1960. Hencher, Skipper, and Cyril are responsible, at least indirectly, for the deaths of several characters.

Yet Hawkes's attachment to these post-1960 narrators depends more upon their function as storytellers than their diabolical intelligences, and so, though the sadism and authoritarianism that result in rebelliousness and survival persist, authorial involvement shifts its main ground. Like involvement through the diabolical intelligence, involvement through the storyteller becomes progressively more disguised. Hawkes's definite, acknowledged link to Zizendorf and Slyter evolves into his indefinite, unacknowledged link to Skipper and Cyril.

During *The Cannibal* prologue, Zizendorf admits, "I was forced to leave the town for a short time and while away I made a compromise. For I have told our story." This awareness of being an author outside the novel is matched by awareness of being an editor inside, where his "fingers were too blunt to punch the keys" and he publishes his Indictment. Amateur historian, inept editor, fanatical propagandist, Zizendorf parodies Hawkes.

So does Slyter, whose "sleazy character and cheap column afforded . . . perhaps the best opportunity for dramatizing the evil inherent in the world of *The Lime Twig*." [57] He plays two parodying roles, sportswriter and chorus. Both are important because the journalist-commentator stands for Hawkes's professional opposite, reporting what has happened, telescoping what will happen, introducing people, and prophesying. As authoritarian Zizendorf-Hawkes impose their messages, bewildered Slyter-Hawkes record their investigations. The novelist-dictator becomes the novelist-policeman: "The detectives represent law and order, or the baffled and banal mind at large. Specifically, and along with Sidney Slyter, they may be seen as images of the absurd and lonely author himself." [58]

Involvement through fictional analogues eventually displaced involvement through fictional antipodes. Like Zizendorf and Slyter, the narrator keeps his raconteur role before the reader during *Second Skin*, concluding the first chapter, "on to the high lights of my naked history," and the last, "this final flourish of my own hand." Unlike them, however, Skipper possesses Hawkes's artistic imagination; he assigns mythico-literary names and juxtaposes literary genres to give the book its time and timelessness, its place and placelessness paradoxes. What might be described as a dramatic monologue, a highly organized explanation, he calls a vision, a hymn, a confession. Skipper's subject is recollected in tranquillity. It requires periodic clarification: "Miranda will have to wait while I turn to a still more distant past. . . . But first my afternoon in the swamp."

Skipper and the other post-1960 narrators speak in more distinctive voices than their predecessors, yet they too lack autonomy. Hawkes's comment on Zizendorf—"the language is mine pretty much"—and on Slyter—"His language is pretty good. After all, it's a version of mine"—also applies to them, for Hawkes, who creates "my own authorial visions of what I take to be reality," does not portray "the psychic states of the characters" (Interview). There is a difference, nonetheless, between language as self-parody and language as self-expression, between the storyteller as anti-artist and the storyteller as artist. Hawkes implicitly criticizes Zizendorf and Slyter when they rationalize, but allows Hencher, Skipper, and Cyril to do so with impunity. He even seems to endorse the inaccurate adjectives Skipper uses in describing himself: harmless, sanguine, serene, graceful, unblemished, fearless, devoted, courageous, relentless.

Hawkes has admitted sharing the criminal or rebellious mentality. Although this satanic posturing did not produce the authorial-authoritarian detachment he hoped for, it did produce the compassion generated by the reversal of artistic sympathy associated with Flannery O'Connor and Nathanael West. Hawkes's compassion toward his pre-1960 narrators occurred regardless of their viciousness because he considered their criminality and rebelliousness directed toward survival. After 1960 sympathy became empathy; and since then a more consciously optimistic, more unconsciously subjective Hawkes has introduced narrators who have combined artistic and sexual creativity.

Hawkes acknowledged a discrepancy between his and the reader's reaction to these post-1960 narrators when he called Hencher sympathetic despite anyone else's impression. Having granted him certain liabilities, he emphasized Hencher's virtues. Yet, for many readers, the faults of Hencher, Skipper, and Cyril outweigh their virtues and contain much of the cruelty and tyranny of their satanic and sadistic predecessors.

Earl Rovit finds Hawkes his own "real protagonist . . . fighting fiercely to reconcile the raging ambivalences in himself." [59] Hawkes said:

I find paradox everywhere. On the one hand, my fiction depends on a kind of cold, detached, authoritarian stance which I could think of as puritanical, but insofar as the fiction is personal it is so only in the sense that I'm interested in destroying puritanism, overcoming puritanical morality. The very subject I'm trying to overcome provides the emotional stance necessary to do the writing in the first place (Interview).

Hawkes's conflict over puritanism, which may be viewed as a conflict between Eros and Thanatos, is dramatized through his narrators. Nowhere is this conflict more vivid and the author more involved than in *Second Skin:*

I wanted to use some of the fictional methods that I have become increasingly aware of—mainly the first-person narrator—so I used a first-person narrator who is a fifty-nine-year-old ex-naval Lieutenant, Junior Grade, a rather ineffectual man, who comes out of a world of suicide—his father committed suicide, his wife committed suicide. Finally the drama in the novel, the conflict in the novel, is the narrator's effort to prevent his daughter's suicide—he is not successful, she dies. However, he himself undergoes all kinds of tribulations and violations and by the end of the novel, I think we do have, in effect, a survivor. This is the first time, I think, in my fiction that there is something affirmative. In other words, even I got very much involved in the life-force versus death. The life and death in the novel go on as a kind of equal contest, until the very end, when a newborn baby, perhaps the narrator's, is taken to a cemetery on a tropical island, on an imaginary island, really, taken to a cemetery on All Saints' Eve with the candles lighted on the graves and so on. And out of this, I think, does come a sort of continuing life. The novel is about a bumbler, an absurd man, sometimes reprehensible, sometimes causing the difficulties, the dilemmas, he gets in—but ending with some kind of inner strength that allows him to live.[60]

Like Hencher, Skipper possesses several character faults Hawkes recognizes. Like Hencher too, his virtues, which

include paternal commitment and inner strength, override
these faults in spite of *Second Skin*'s world of suicide, tribulations, and violations. The affirmative outcome derives from
a newborn baby and from a narrator-survivor.

Nearly all the *Studies in Second Skin* [61] stress this
affirmation in the novel. William R. Robinson writes:
Skipper's "triumph consists . . . of simply letting life have
its way with him . . . helping it joyously reach its proper
end, the creation of further life, by begetting a child and
breeding, via his benign control, his herd of cows" (pp.
67–68); Stephen G. Nichols, Jr.: " 'The Nearest Cemetery'
shares *Second Skin*'s preoccupation with death, but the
Barber can never boast with Skipper that he has finished
with death, nor does the story assert the theme of birth and
rebirth (the 'Second Skin' theme) as the ultimate triumph
over death" (p. 71); and Albert J. Guerard: "Hawkes makes
a very clear affirmative statement of theme. *Second Skin* is a
vision of the will to survive death and abomination and of
the power to move from impotence to fertility" (p. 94).

Among these positive interpretations, "Awakening
Paradise" (pp. 52–63) by Lucy Frost contains the fullest,
most persuasive argument. She believes the "battle against
the forces of death" represents "the central battle throughout Hawkes's fiction." In *Second Skin,* Skipper, "a self-
professed, all-embracing lover," serves Eros or Life. His
"land journey across the American continent" toward the
Atlantic island geographically shows him trying to save
Cassandra. But, as was the case with father and wife, he
cannot prevent her suicide because Miranda (Sycorax) and
Captain Red, who serve Thanatos or Death, take control.
They embody "those demonic forces" producing destruction and disintegration which dominate Western civilization and wartime America and which make the protagonist
an impotent victim. According to Miss Frost, second skins

are unavailing protective devices. "Wind becomes a metaphor for powers controlling the external world"; escape is the only answer. Like betrayed Prospero, Skipper goes on another journey and arrives at an Edenic island, where "the contrast between the two [cemetery] pilgrimages repeats the contrast between the two voyages." Here, "in a post-cultural environment," Hawkes treats his original world comically, rendering it non-violent, innocuous. Reborn, Skipper now exercises control, "transforms the events of life into the rituals marking the forms that constitute a culture." Coitus is "the center of a religious celebration that takes the form of a fertility cult. . . . Love must bring life; coitus, pregnancy." This affects Catalina Kate, the cows, and even the reader; hopefully, all will be impregnated by "the seeds of life through the artificial method that is art."

Such analyses, no matter how well reasoned or perceptive, accept Hawkes's storyteller at face value. A shore patrol officer with the Good Conduct Medal, Skipper professes knightly-saintly qualities while he endures the self-inflicted deaths of Papa, Gertrude, and Cassandra; the mutiny of Tremlow; and the nefarious plans of Miranda, Captain Red, and Jomo. His struggles are Manichean, as when he as accolyte confronts Tremlow as devil or when he as Eros subdues Miranda as Thanatos. Keeper of the cross, lover of life, Skipper, the Artificial Inseminator, redeems Papa, the Undertaker. He participates in two parallel actions, the one, gestation and birth, superseding the other, degeneration and death. That Catalina Kate bears her child on All Saints' Day—figuratively, New Year's Eve—seems to confirm the life victory of her master.

Because this external or ideational pattern is undercut by an internal or human pattern, however, both Hawkes and those critics who take their position from paternal commitment, inner strength, and continuing life are guilty of the Intentional Fallacy, "the error of judging the success and meaning of a work of art by the author's expressed or ostensible intention in producing it." [62] Hawkes, if not the critics, may be forgiven, since unwitting personal involvement has made him overoptimistic toward his novels as well as oversympathetic toward his narrators.

Unlike most of the critics, Hawkes does voice some misgivings about being so positive. *Second Skin* has "barbs . . . hidden beneath the flowers," and he describes its spokesman as ineffectual, absurd, reprehensible. Skipper reveals another, even more damaging handicap: "The extent to which he is unaware of his powerful relationship to his daughter is one way we could think of Skipper as an imperceptive narrator" (Interview). This imperceptiveness is responsible for the partly conscious, partly unconscious irony governing *Second Skin*.

There occur remarkable contradictions between what the narrator says of himself and what he does. Skipper calls himself courageous, but during "The Brutal Act" chapter he is tardy and ineffective. Near the outset, he issues the boy Tremlow a timid order to replace a tarpaulin, then salutes and goes aft, once again managing "to avoid his deliberate signs of insubordination." Later Sonny reports that the lifeboats have been tampered with and the small arms stolen. Skipper reacts by spending the day reading. At the sight of Tremlow stowing a box away, he falls asleep. That night he learns of the mutineers' party and uncovers further evidence of the mutiny but, when confronting the ringleader at the helm, Skipper prevents Sonny's resistance. Eventually, he even allows Tremlow to flee, reports the mutineers missing in action, and tells his commander that the boats were lost in a storm. There are other evasions of reality. While Tremlow pummels him, he still misses "the idea, the plan"; while the mutineers pile on him, "a purpose in that struggle" still escapes him.

In the following scene—the discovery of Fernandez's body—he refuses to scrutinize another victim's face because that other victim may be Tremlow. Here doubts emerge about the "unblemished" quality Skipper thinks of himself as having. He looks at Fernandez's mutilated corpse, throws up, and speaks to a blonde prostitute. She tearfully describes how a sailor who stopped by earlier slept with her just before confessing complicity in the crime. Although Skipper gives the prostitute considerable sympathy, he too is aroused by violence, for, subsequently, he kisses Cassandra's sixteen-year-old guard, the scrubgirl Sissy: "Her mouth tasted like old wax paper but it was the kiss of my life."

That kiss is an example of the profound sexual problem behind the narrator's contradictions: Skipper's attraction to pubescent girls. At the high school dance, he is not ashamed to peer through their jerseys or imagine their panties. The little buttocks were already corrupted, he decides, steadying himself against Chloris (clitoris), whose face communicates "Dionysian incest" and whose partner's reprimand inspires a blush over "the realization I had been squeezing her little thin rounded shoulder." Later, the "little girl guide" Bubbles, "child of chewing gum kisses and plump young body sweetly dusted with baby talc," entices Skipper outside. There he savors her scent and holds her hand; when she retreats, he wonders "whether or not I would dare ask Bubbles for a kiss." Adolescence immediately avenges itself on this adult violator as his guide leads him into a snowball fight near the cemetery where children are buried and students make love.

Old Ariel in sneakers pursues nymphets but fears women. His archenemy, Miranda, is initially encountered through her "black brassiere that dangled as large and stark as an albatross." That and other allusions to breasts and nipples recur, indicating an inordinate horror of the "terrible mammalian concussion." Miranda joins masculine power with feminine promiscuity, a combination Skipper dreads. She betrays him by arranging Cassandra's seduction.

Skipper identifies with the cuckold Menelaus and sees women as treacherous; they come to symbolize the single most overwhelming force of universal evil. Women, in turn, despise him. He quotes, then comments on, one of his wife's letters: " 'You are going to hate me, Edward,' she wrote, 'at least you won't deny me hate, will you?' But she was wrong. Because the further she went downhill the more I cared. And Gertrude was no match for my increasing tolerance." When Skipper goes upstairs after Miranda's first unsuccessful "pass," he finds a ketchup-splattered dummy "at the head of my bed . . . dressed . . . in my naval uniform so that the artificial bosom swelled my white tunic and the artificial pregnancy of the padded belly puffed out the broad front of my official duck pants . . . hapless effigy of my disfigured self."

Miranda and Gertrude might well feel that their hostility was a reaction to something in the victim's character. Whether this is passivity or effeminacy, it adds up to impotence. Yet they do not lash out against that alone. Skipper and Sonny share a latent homosexual relationship and play "mammy" to Pixie. Skipper, confessing "had I been born my mother's daughter instead of son—and the thought is not . . . improbable," prefers "large and innocent Iphigenia" to "muscular and self-willed Clytemnestra." He chooses an effeminate husband, Fernandez, for Cassandra and a masculine sparring partner, Tremlow, for himself. That Tremlow detests Skipper's homosexual nature seems clear from their fight, when, sporting the grass skirt, the younger sailor rapes the older. His sexually ambivalent dance had inspired the mutiny and was a parody of female betrayal.

Perhaps Gertrude drinks and cheats because her husband does not satisfy her. Perhaps Miranda, Cassandra's surrogate-mother during the Gentle Island episodes, leads Cassandra away from Skipper to virile men so that, free of his covert incest, she may enjoy overt sex. They get along very well. Skipper says, "Cassandra was Miranda's shadow," and Miranda says, "Like mother, like daughter."

In her father's Christian imagination, Cassandra is part Eve and part Mary. He uses the word "schizophrenic" when discussing "the young-old figure of my Cassandra." To him, she is both "teen-age bomb" and "queen." The first gives her the appearance of a drum majorette, a cheerleader, and the second the appearance of a young matron. Playing queen—a role that exists solely in Skipper's imagination—Cassandra represents the Blessed Virgin Mary. Will bomb destroy queen or queen bomb? he speculates, meaning will whore destroy virgin or virgin whore?

"I would love them both," Skipper contends, yet he unconsciously prizes bomb over queen. He calls twenty-five-year-old Cassandra "my child courtesan" with the body "of a child in puberty." They are "in the middle of no romance," but at the tattooer's she refers to him as "my boy friend" and on the bus as "my last blind date." Such courtship situations and images pervade the scenes at the high school gymnasium and the Chinatown café. During both, Skipper expresses concern about Cassandra's vulgar attire, especially the green taffeta dress with the "bow that bound her buttocks." And, during both, he imagines himself protecting Cassandra from intoxicated servicemen. Skipper is a zealous suitor as well as a jealous rival. At the café, Hawkes's "big soft flower of fatherhood" wishes he were an anonymous seaman escorting the girl; at the gymnasium, the bomb grants the first dance to Jomo, not Skipper, so Skipper cuts in. His sexual attraction to infantile Cassandra is unmistakable. At the gymnasium, he caresses her knee, hip, and breasts; at the café, he considers whirling her around to make her skirts rise.

Later Skipper is strangely paralyzed while Captain Red seduces Cassandra aboard the *Peter Poor*. Although he has pointed out that slacks would have been "more appropriate to a boat" than a full skirt, his paternal objection is half-hearted. Skipper suspects the crew's motives, yet, feeling ill, meekly allows Jomo to usher him below. The sight of Captain Red and Cassandra flirting reminds Skipper of the blonde prostitute and causes a fit of vomiting. Then the boy Bub hits him with a tire iron, which he fails to block, and afterward he watches Captain Red's seduction until Bub hits him again. Skipper repeatedly experiences intimations about this passivity. He senses that it grows "out of the intuitive resources of my destructive sympathy," a destructive sympathy implied earlier by references casting Captain Red as Skipper's alter ego. Like him, Red is a large, bald-pated, ocean-going widower. Skipper possesses the Good Conduct Medal and nicknames ironically suggesting control. The captain has "the medal the Coast Guard had given him for heroism" and authority over disciples and vessel. This authority extends to his sex-life, for he has produced two sons and copulated with Miranda. The father's alter ego thus becomes the daughter's lover.

Covert homosexual and overt nympholept, incestuous Skipper derives vicarious pleasure from other mock rapes involving Cassandra. The first takes place when they are stranded on their cross-country bus ride. Three AWOL soldiers of Company C for Cain approach, strip, and, "each

one ready to have his turn," kiss the blue Madonna, while
Skipper trembles, smiles, sweats, and squeezes her hand.
The second happens at the high school dance. There, Bub,
Jomo, and Captain Red "began cutting in on each
other . . . serving as outriders for each other . . .
taking turns. There, Skipper, observing Jomo's hook
in Cassandra's bow and his leg between hers, might have
intervened had not the belly-bumping contest commenced.
An even clearer instance of mock rape occurs during her
honeymoon, where father rather than husband behaves
like the groom. Skipper urges Fernandez to proffer flowers
and Fernandez often scolds him, answering his
father-in-law's admonition, "Courage," by declaring, "Fernandez is no innocent," terming his father-in-law's phrase,
"Short but passionate," "Indelicate," and correcting his
father-in-law's slip, "my little bride at last!" Other remarks
made by Skipper are revealing. He wishes that he "hadn't
already kissed the bride," that the bride and the groom
"could sit in back," that the tiny glass contained an aphrodisiac. Hawkes's innocence-lust motif appears here. Before arriving at Honeymoon Hide-Away, Cassandra, wearing a white dress and a silver fertility charm, is compared to
the "plastic Madonna screwed to the dashboard." But later
allusions invert this. The hotel, which has been a brothel,
includes a bar displaying "the plump naked bodies of young
Victorian women carved in bas-relief" and a girlie calendar
above several romantic jukebox titles. Leaving the hotel,
Skipper comes across another house of pleasure associated
with past wantonness, an abandoned movie theater, and
discovers tickets for an old film starring Rita Hayworth "as
the unfaithful mistress of a jealous killer."

Skipper admits being wrong about Fernandez only
after proof of Fernandez's homosexuality. His whole effort
is supposedly to save his daughter, but errors in judgment

recur. He delays informing Cassandra about the Fernandez tragedy and suppresses many details. "Those two or three months . . . made all the difference," he concedes. That information could have prevented her suicide and so could refusal to board the *Peter Poor:* "There was a chance for Cassandra up to the very moment she swung her foot gaily over the rail . . . there was no chance . . . after." An apprehensive Skipper nevertheless embarks, then says had he realized what he eventually did, pride and innocence would have dictated the same action. Less critical miscalculations disturb the reader. Why, for example, does Skipper allow himself to be propelled into a belly-bumping contest he regards as obscene, becoming so engrossed that Jomo may abduct Cassandra unnoticed?

She expresses through her withdrawals, reprimands, and betrayals a resentment toward her father evident in other adolescents he encounters. Cassandra avoids him, particularly when physical contact is involved. During the bus ride, she retreats from his sprawling thigh and during the high school dance she remains stiff and aloof when he replaces Jomo as her partner. In contrast are Cassandra's affectionate responses to various other males. She fingers the chest of one Kissin' Bandit and notifies Skipper, "Nobody wants to kiss you." On the *Peter Poor* she cooperates with Captain Red but humiliates her father, and in the lighthouse, where she spends "the last six or eight hours of her life with Jomo," she ignores his desperate entreaties.

The girl's most extreme hostility erupts at the tattooer's. There Skipper undergoes physical pain for Cassandra, whose revenge strikes deeper than merely inflicting bodily torture. Her eyes look hard and radiate "a bright new triumphant color" as the tattooer finishes a green "Fernandez" above Skipper's heart. This tattoo could sig-

nify an affinity between homosexual husband and effemi-
nate father or the jealousy and real desires of the latter.
Whatever the meaning, Skipper can never forget the green
lizard "exposed and crawling on my breast," a curse which
Cassandra shows Captain Red and which even Floating
Island sunshine cannot completely obliterate.

Skipper is implicated as definitely in Cassandra's death
as he was in Gertrude's. Outside the lighthouse, he wonders
if he were "the unwitting tinder that started the blaze," and
before boarding the *Peter Poor*, he muses, "accomplice,
father, friend, traveling companion, yes, old chaperon, but
lover and destroyer too." During a moment of self-
awareness, Skipper admits edging Cassandra (and Gertrude) toward suicide. This pattern the barber had consciously enacted in the earlier version where he loved the
Princess from afar and then killed her. Skipper's parallel
performance, conscious or not, makes him more sinister
than Hawkes's delineation of "a bumbler, an absurd man,
sometimes reprehensible, sometimes causing the difficulties, the dilemmas he gets in." Like the narrator of
"The Nearest Cemetery," the narrator of *Second Skin* com-
mits murder, even though the act is indirect.

His entanglement with death began when his father
was a small-town mortician, his home an undertaking parlor, his family's car an old hearse. The father died by suicide
just before the mother mysteriously succumbed, extending
the boy's "knowledge of death as a lurid truth." He regards
the father as "Death himself," and asks if he, Skipper, is not
"simply one of those little black seeds of death?" Having
inherited Papa's morbid preoccupation, he becomes obsessive. A case in point is the recurrent hallucination he experiences about his mother and a driver wearing "a white
cap and driving coat, great eyeless goggles and a black

muffler." This driver, or Death, operates the limousine at Gertrude's funeral.

Skipper habitually connects death and sex. His daughter's face, which resembles "a little death mask of Pascal" during the Chinatown scene, remains a "little death-mask" during the bus ride. The expression "blue tit" initiates and concludes winter nightmares; only the bathroom talisman, *Wake with a Loving Thought./Work with a Happy Thought./Sleep with a Gentle Thought*," can ward off such horrors. After Jomo has abducted Cassandra from the high school dance, Skipper trudges home along a "wintry road . . . littered with the bodies of dead birds."

*Second Skin* borrowed many "Nearest Cemetery" settings and properties—island, church, lighthouse, clapboard house, gasoline pumps, orange pop, Crooked Finger Rock, rowboat—but none more significant than the graveyard. Cemetery symbolism that connotes the burial place of the barber's past in the story is expanded in the novel. Cemeteries become the dominant death metaphor. They are sometimes alluded to and sometimes visited, but always they suggest masculine impotence and feminine promiscuity. At Gertrude's grave, Skipper deposits the old man's sword; at Cassandra's, a grandchild's fetus.

To understand why he connects death and sex is to understand the psyche of the narrator. Child-accomplice during his father's suicide, Skipper confesses that the shot that killed everything may have been induced by misguided cello-playing. Involvement in the suicide was doubtless unavoidable for this son of Death. Yet, because the suicide represents the traumatic experience that rendered him impotent, it made him both victim and victimizer. Henceforth, Skipper forswears reality, refusing to explore motives or to act even upon things he comprehends. Ego becomes egotism; the man, the mask. Consequently, he never matures—a fact demonstrated by his love life. He pursues nymphets, including Cassandra, because he fears women and does not realize that sexual inadequacy, like all inadequacy, spells death. Skipper links death to promiscuity, but the reader may link it to impotence.

The negative interpretation of *Second Skin* dismisses the Floating Island as a refuge from time and place. Evil and mortality persist in the water wheel, missionary madness, boils, the swamp, the iguana, and "the fella in the grave." Ultimately, Skipper feels triumphant over death, but he is a leader with an illiterate following, a master with an adolescent mistress, a creator with an amorous pipette. The Artificial Inseminator appears to be insensible of the irony of his new role. Nor does he sense the irony when the steer, his namesake Edward, vainly mounts the cow Sweet Phyllis. Himself a steer, he probably did not impregnate her human counterpart, Cataline Kate.

All Hawkes's first-person narrators except Hencher manage to survive, and, since that is the goal, both the negative and affirmative views of *Second Skin* would admit that the survival of Skipper is crucial. But though the affirmative view, interpreting the book as essentially straightforward, makes Eros victorious over Thanatos, the negative view, interpreting the book as essentially ironic, makes Thanatos victorious over Eros. The first view stresses the narrator's intelligence, revealed desires, statements; the second, his imperceptiveness, concealed wishes, behavior. The first view, based upon authorial commentary, emphasizes the external or ideational pattern; the second, based upon authorial involvement, stresses the internal or human pattern. Instead of diminishing *Second Skin*, however, the discrepancy between what Hawkes intends and achieves, like the discrepancy between what Skipper says and does, supplies texture. Taken at the conscious level positively or at the unconscious level negatively, the two designs retain their coherence and unity. The resulting tension produces ambiguity rather than obscurity because the author, if not most of his critics, appreciates paradox.

# 6

# Sweetness and Blood

Hawkes called L'Anse aux Epines, "the most southerly tip" of Grenada, West Indies, "our paradise spot and the terrain that gave off *Second Skin*." In another letter, he elaborated: "Incidentally, the swamp used to lie immediately behind the little crescent of beach below the 'great' house—the beach that used to have a small jetty and a few dangerous stinging trees at its edge. But I think they filled in the swamp when they put up a bunch of hotel-cottages there." His next novel, *The Blood Oranges*, also has Jamesian "solidity of specification." According to him, "I began *The Blood Oranges* in Vence (near Nice) and worked on it for a few more months in Tolon, Greece, which you may know is down near Nauphplion (sp?) and Epidaurus (sp?) in the Peloponnessus (sp??), so the world of *The Blood Oranges* is mixed Mediterranean (sp?)," and "Yes, the Roman cistern in *Blood Oranges* was actually located in a small much-overlooked temple on a ridge above Epidaurus, where we spent many a lovely sunset being pleased and renewed." [63] This mixed Mediterranean land-

scape is as mythical as *Second Skin*'s Floating Island. Fiona
asks if Cyril knows where they are and he replies,
"Sure . . . we're in Illyria." But the geographical area of
the Adriatic coast will not suffice for the setting of *The Blood
Oranges*, as Cyril "is simply trying to designate the power,
beauty, fulfillment, the possibility that is evident in any
actual scene we exist in. . . . Illyria doesn't exist unless
you bring it into being." [64]

    *The Blood Oranges* (1971) modifies and extends tech-
niques and preoccupations that have been with Hawkes
since the writing of *Charivari* and *The Cannibal*. Evolving
from several antecedent novels, it resembles *Second Skin*.
*The Blood Oranges* is a simplified version of the latter as *The
Owl* is a simplified version of *The Cannibal*. Both sequels
represent attempts to clarify their dense and difficult origi-
nals.

    Combining sweetness and blood, the title of *The Blood
Oranges* is paradoxical: "It means that the blood is real but
also sweet; it means that no sweetness is ephemeral but on
the contrary possesses all the life-drive seriousness of the
rich black flow of blood itself. It suggests wound invading
desire, desire 'containing' agony." Hawkes's desire-agony
dichotomy receives additional significance through the
chastity belt, "a central image in *The Blood Oranges*" and
"central to everything I've written":


That is, my fiction is generally an evocation of the nightmare or
terroristic universe in which sexuality is destroyed by law, by
dictum, by human perversity, by contraption, and it is this destruction of human sexuality which I have attempted to portray
and confront in order to be true to human fear and to human
ruthlessness, but also in part to evoke its opposite, the moment of
freedom from constriction, constraint, death.[65]

Paradox marked the initial struggle between Eros and Thanatos in *The Lime Twig* and reached an apotheosis during *Second Skin* where Skipper combines both. Paradox is also markedly present in *The Blood Oranges*. There things are simplified by schematization: "the two sides of Skipper" become Cyril (Eros) and Hugh (Thanatos). "They dramatize the polarity of what we have been talking about in the light of religious experience and authorial impulse. On the one hand, I am darkly committed to the puritan ethic. On the other, I detest it and want to destroy it. And in crude terms Cyril and Hugh represent that polarity" (Interview). This schematization sacrifices complexity of characterization to produce a conflict more intelligible to the reader. Although the conflict is clearer than before, the old ambiguities persist.

Cyril and Hugh stand for the opposition of purity and puritanism, love and idealism, and life against death. Their mythological associations demonstrate this. Hugh has the "rigid outstretched white legs of the Christ" and his "pointed ears, hard eyes, bitter mouth" suggest a resemblance to both Saint Peter and Saint Paul. Cyril, who ironically calls Hugh "great Pan," is a white bull, a headless god, a satyr, a flower god, and thus symbolizes vaguely potent pagan deities. When the goat-girl joins them, Cyril's Aphrodite, faunlike Fiona, advises him, "Kiss her, baby. She probably thinks you're some kind of god." And, indeed, he does bear a name that signifies "lord."

Images, particularly those involving clothes and the human body, are important definitions of character in *The Blood Oranges*. A pattern posing nakedness against its reverse emerges from a multitude of such references. For example, the "immodest" underwear, nightwear, and sportswear worn by Cyril, Fiona, and Catherine contrast with Hugh's "modest" tweed jacket, turtleneck shirt, bell-bottom trousers, long-sleeved cotton shirt, jersey, and pea jacket. Holding the recently discovered chastity belt, Hugh "exposed to us the pink and pointed nakedness of his partial arm. But nonetheless he refused to strip off his denim pants and accompany our nude trio."

Clothing also reveals the kinds and uses of color prevalent in *The Blood Oranges*. "Yellow was Fiona's color" and gold Cyril's, but both share Catherine's affinity for white. Just as their casual dress contrasts to the heavy vestments of Hugh, their light tones are antithetical to his blacks and blues. This opposition includes the human body when Hawkes contrasts Catherine's amber eyes and Cyril's blond hair to Hugh's black eyes, hair, and beard. J. E. Circlot identifies "warm 'advancing' colours" like "red, orange, yellow and, by extension, white" with "processes of assimilation, activity and intensity" and "cold, 'retreating' colours" like "blue, indigo, violet and, by extension, black" with "processes of dissimilation, passivity and debilitation." [66] All the people representing the Life-Force in *The Blood Oranges* have red clothing: Fiona's pink shirt and rosy shorts, Catherine's maroon-colored shorts and red sash, Cyril's magenta trunks and maroon-colored dressing gown.

Hugh's sexual regression, implied in his clothing and its color, is made explicit by his ritualistic behavior, epitomized when Cyril overhears him repeating, "Don't be afraid of Daddy Bear," as a "sad and presumptuous appeal" to Catherine. The narrator conjectures that this monogamous song, "stolen in desperation from the vocabulary of the cheapest myth of childhood," originated during the honeymoon, and that subsequently Hugh "had spent all the nights of his marriage fishing for the love of his wife with the hook of a nursery persona."

Cyril's own rituals, because they celebrate sexual extension, are the most positive Hawkes has described. The grape-tasting scene is typical. Master of ceremonies, Cyril supervises it, placing the participants shoulder to shoulder, giving instructions, going first, appointing Catherine second. Hugh recognizes the game's sensual nature as he self-consciously exclaims, "Nipples, boy." He resents the physical contact between his wife and Cyril. At the beginning, Cyril terms the arbor a "place for the bedding down of lovers"; at the end, he muses, "So much . . . for the viscera of the cornucopia."

Doubles drawn from their Mediterranean hosts further dramatize these Anglo-Saxon opposites. When they bury Hugh's old black dog, an animal that resembles it leaps forward with a shepherd that looks like Hugh. The bony arm of this black and white personage is similar to the one arm of his Anglo-Saxon counterpart. To both, only death matters.

Just as the death-oriented shepherd of the burial scene symbolizes Hugh, the life-oriented old man of the wedding scene stands for Cyril. Hawkes emphasizes the old man's vitality and vulgarity: agile, disreputable, impish, energetic, indomitable, he has a "shirt ripped open to the waist," "partially unbuttoned trousers," and "unspent passion . . . hanging down." Significantly, this friendly guide resists the priest but accepts Cyril and Catherine, whose past he read and "whose spiritual relationship he somehow shared." They "had come under the aegis of the little crouching goat-faced man half naked at the end of the day."

The burial and the wedding are rituals, one negative and one positive. The burial or "makeshift ceremonial affair" employs a familiar procession: Hugh and Fiona lead the death party as pallbearers, he enacting his game, his formal plan, his funeral fantasy, and she her role of "beau-

tiful dry-eyed priestess"; then, in the middle, come
Catherine and the children, followed by Cyril in the rear
with the Byzantine cross. When they deposit Hugh's dog
where Hugh masturbated earlier, the shepherd, thinking
their "small, black, thickly ornamented" coffin contains an
infant, crosses himself.

The wedding, executed during the boat-launching
spectacle according to Hawkes (Interview), is another pro-
cessional. Before they "were thrust . . . on opposite sides
of the narrow street," Cyril admits Catherine offered
nothing, and, after the boat slides between them and they
trail the crowd, he observes, "She and I were simply the two
halves of the ancient fruit together but unjoined." Communication commences, however, once they become involved in helping to push the boat downhill. Cyril mutters,
"Starting over." Though primitive—gesticulating priest,
archaic deity, sacred wood, blood, old instruments—the
launching occurs "for the sake of Catherine, me, and for
one . . . ageless village elder" (the old man). It reminds
Cyril of a wedding, what with its festive air and life-
emblems like the golden fish and white flowers on the boat's
white prow. The old man proposes a toast and towers
nakedly above his disciples amid "thick erotic color."
Thanatos conducts the burial ritual, Eros the wedding.

In *The Blood Oranges* external nature also dramatizes
the opposition between Cyril and Hugh. It is neither entirely hostile as in *The Beetle Leg* nor indifferent as in *The
Lime Twig* but ambivalent as in *Second Skin*. Surrounding the
*twin* villas, positive aspects (golden glen, fruit trees, flowers)
are mixed with negative aspects (funeral cypresses, crab-
grass, dead gardens, gloomy pines, brambles, weeds,
thorns). A similar ambivalence characterizes the beach
where the four adults exchange partners occasionally. At
their sacred spot nearby, Cyril feels that the ominous dis-

tance "belied . . . lyricism, grape-bespattered joys of
love." Then, incongruous yet apt, an eagle descends to
proclaim "the breath of dead kings" *and* the sunrise. The
black and silver sky grows orange, the cold air turns warm,
and the hills, formerly dark burial mounds, disclose a clear
pattern.

More than in any novel since *The Beetle Leg*, external
nature in *The Blood Oranges* reflects character and psychic
states. Cyril and Fiona have better luck raising morning
glories than Hugh, whose death-orientation is illustrated by
the funeral cypresses. Prior to Catherine's partial cure,
Cyril notices a "rotting arbor . . . cluster of dead grapes,"
and, afterward, an "arbor thick [with] . . . hanging ten-
drils." He has wooed Catherine, conducted the grape-
tasting ritual, faced Hugh there. And there, among
hymeneal grapes, was the "quiet and appropriate place for
our reunion."

A wall of funeral cypresses separates the twin villas and
a clothesline connects them. Both dwellings appear deso-
late, dilapidated, and old, but the one that Hugh and
Catherine occupy suggests "transient lives," and the one
Cyril and Fiona share "harmonious life." Upper and lower
worlds reminiscent of those introduced in *The Cannibal*
during Stella's honeymoon are also juxtaposed. The upper
world sanctuary where Catherine convalesces has cheerful
colors and "is antithetical to the brambles and broken tiles
of the primitive landscape" below. Each week Cyril leaves
the gloom and darkness of the funeral cypresses and coastal
village for "the sudden light, peace, charm of this walled
sanctuary." He may travel freely between the two worlds,
whereas Hugh may not.

Hawkes opposes lower world town and fortress to
countryside and villas. That Hugh's studio is in the town
establishes an affinity between him and the dark town,

which is primitive and decayed. The town's black canal has some of these same attributes. Its noxiousness is stressed by the use of adjectives like polluted, fetid, pestilential, viscous, excremental. From the "historically significant canal" emanates a lethal atmosphere associated with the aboriginal savages once festering there.

Religious and military images keep the past before the reader. Cyril's seaside chapel on the "small timeless island" contains a cross, and the medieval church beside the cemetery holds "all the effluvium of devotion and religious craftsmanship." Here, in a dark, empty, barbarous, humorless, and cold environment, Fiona and Hugh steal a wooden arm, Catherine collapses during Hugh's funeral, and Cyril looks at sketches showing the conflict between Eros and Thanatos. "A feeling of ancient violence" permeates the church, partly because the "windows were cut through those deep walls as if for arrows, lances, pikes and small cannon."

The fortress across the water also serves as a symbol of psychic states. When Cyril, Fiona, Hugh, and Catherine face its dread "shape of history" joined "by wind and light and hands," Cyril thinks the fortress ominous. Later it is described as hard, unhealthy, damp, and treacherous. Since their quest, which will explore "the dark caves of the heart," fulfills Hugh's premonition about the chastity belt, the fortress becomes an analogue for him. Cyril, who prefers lyrical landscapes, links such dismal places to Hugh's "secret self," his "regressive nature." Both fortress and Hugh represent the desolation and constriction inherited from a religio-martial past that has produced the stunted sexuality evident in the "indecipherable . . . sex legends" Hugh ignores and the "unreadable injunctions against frivolity and sex" Fiona examines at the church. The

church, with its narrow windows, seems to have military
overtones, and the penitential fortress religious ones. At
the fortress Fiona resembles "some lady saint stretched
head to toe on her tomb" and Hugh "tipped [the chastity
belt] onto the alter of the fallen pediment."

Hugh's studio emphasizes past primitiveness too.
Characterized by "monastic gloom" and "thick walls," it is a
crude, dark, medieval cell. Hawkes claims that "Hugh
doesn't mean to kill himself" there:

He means to undergo a partial hanging in order to experience
sexual release, but he slips and thus accidentally dies. I meant the
death of Hugh in a sense to trick the reader into thinking of it as a
moral judgment on the multiple relationships—but to me it is not.
Hugh's death is thoroughly absurd (Interview).

Accidental or intentional, Hugh's death occurs in an appropriate setting, for the studio overlooking the canal
aligns him with the retarded natives. Like the ancient barbarians he and the townspeople reincarnate, he comes
"from beyond the mountains." Even his motor-
bus—"Derelict, obviously painted and repaired end-
lessly by lazy, unskilled workers"—confirms his bond to
their descendants, an unspecified Mediterranean people.

Suffering "from the abnormal attitudes born of the
bad blood carried to this warm coast centuries before from
central Europe," the natives, who have archaic ways and
objects, are hostile, lewd, and violent. Disease ("some congenital rasping respiratory disease"), deformity, and sub-
human physical traits symbolize their psychic disturbances.
Rosella, the most important native, is an illiterate virgin
with "origins . . . in historical darkness" and "blood
determined . . . by one of the barbaric strains." Her
blunt look, animal-like posture, overlapping teeth, green

face, and small eyes reveal this heritage no less than her crow's feet and unappealing wardrobe reveal "the latent old peasant woman already snoring inside."

The book draws repeated physical contrasts between the Mediterranean natives (short, swarthy, clumsy) and the Anglo-Saxon foreigners (tall, fair, graceful). They imply the superiority of the Anglo-Saxons, with the exception of dark, diseased, deformed Hugh (Christian), and the inferiority of the natives, except for the unaccountable old man (pagan). "Godlike," the Anglo-Saxons form a "sacred circle"; "godlike," they congregate near "a sacred wood" or in a "sacred spot."

Cyril's courtship of Mediterranean Rosella parallels his courtship of Anglo-Saxon Catherine. Cyril encounters "Hugh's last peasant nude" during a photographic expedition. Drawn toward though repelled by the girl's incongruous figure, Cyril concludes this episode, "Thanks to Hugh [she] became mine." Mute Rosella covers raw, unshaved legs with thick woolen socks. Nevertheless, Cyril will pay her clandestine visits "when . . . dormancy dissolves"; he feels that she requires "some physical gesture of affection"; he speculates about being Rosella's "mimosa tree as well as her white beast"; he sleeps alone but can hear her snoring; he refers to "absent suitors spurned for me." During both courtships, Cyril is impotent, optimistic, egocentric, while Rosella and Catherine are disinterested, passive, silent. They submit—according to him—but not sexually. His Mediterranean virgin never overcomes a puritanical outlook, however, whereas his Anglo-Saxon mistress does.

So may Meredith, Catherine's daughter and Rosella's other counterpart. Because she exhibits a mind "like her father's," the opposition between Cyril and Meredith reflects the opposition between Cyril and Hugh. Meredith condemns what she thinks of as the adulterous, destructive love of her parents and Fiona and Cyril. She's exemplary of conventional hostility towards law-breaking. She threatens our attitudes toward Cyril, she makes us doubt him or question him at certain moments, she elicits his sadism. She's conscience and comic foil combined (Interview).

Cyril exposes Meredith and her younger sisters, Dolores and Eveline, to a "test" seduction of Catherine. He thereby arouses an antagonism in the children that prefigures the feeling he will provoke in Hugh. Yet, since Meredith's liability is sexual inhibition, not sexual extension, Hugh rather than Cyril represents her adult corrupter. His accusing, complaining, spiteful, introverted, unforgiving, suspicious, fearful, duplicitous offspring, suffering from nosebleed and bearing a vaccination mark, resembles him: "little tight-lipped mouth," "thin white naked shoulders," "little pinched pragmatic face." Her "outgrown childish light green frock" and "sadly modest swimming suit" also attest to inherited inhibitions. Nevertheless, two scenes demonstrate "hope for Meredith." During the white goat incident, she undresses and dances; during the flower crowns incident, she enjoys self-beautification by hiking up her baggy shorts and curling her chopped-off hair. Yet "hope" is not fully justified until the children depart with Fiona after Hugh's death and thus escape Hugh's pernicious influence.

Speaking about *The Blood Oranges*, Hawkes has contended, "I deliberately omitted the past lives of the characters" because "I wanted to create characters in total purity and to deny myself the novelistic easiness of past lives to draw on" (Interview). Vague allusions are made to Cyril's previous life, but only Meredith, Dolores, and Eveline really experience a past. Whereas heredity and environment do not seem to determine the behavior of the Anglo-Saxons, the Mediterraneans are the product of the "bad blood" transmitted to them from their barbaric forebears. In *The Blood Oranges*, then, determinism is racial, the result of a primitive religio-martial heritage. Since a southern people represent Thanatos here but Eros in *Second Skin*, light and dark and north and south stand for positive-negative psychic poles rather than superior-inferior ethnic or geographical groups in Hawkes's work. Spiritually, the Anglo-Saxon Hugh is a Mediterranean and the Mediterranean old man an Anglo-Saxon.

Regardless of elaborate spatial and temporal juxtapositions involving town vs. countryside, upper vs. lower world, time-past vs. time-present, daytime vs. nighttime, sunset vs. sunrise, *The Blood Oranges*, "a visionary fiction" that "only resembles a novel" (Interview), continues Hawkes's movement toward conventional form. It contains forty-two unnumbered, untitled sections ranging from seven lines to thirty-two pages and includes essays on Love, Pain, Marriage, and Virginity, yet the controlling plot or present courtship of Catherine reveals a simplicity rivaling the pattern of Catalina Kate's pregnancy. This controlling plot is overwhelmed by past events:

In other words, the action of the novel is Hugh's resistance to Fiona which climaxes in his forcing the chastity belt upon Catherine which in turn precipitates Cyril's major effort to convince Hugh to accept Fiona's love. But after the argument in the grape arbor, which Cyril wins, there follows a long idyllic period in which the four characters are actually intermingling their loves, as the jacket says. What's left out is that all this time while Hugh is finally knowing Fiona sexually he has nonetheless still been experiencing his own inner solipsized sexual life through his photographs and that dangling rope (Interview).

In *The Blood Oranges*, as in *Second Skin*, time-past, a long adventure terminating a few months before, dominates time-present, not just because past action bulks larger, but because the chronological vocabulary employed shows the present and future continuously metamorphosing into the past. Both vertical and controlling plots have climactic occurrences; yet the present action culminates early when Catherine and Cyril symbolically wed, and the past culminates late when Hugh forces the chastity belt on her. Present action during *The Blood Oranges* (the submission of Catherine to Cyril) *seems* triumphant over past action (the resistance of Hugh to Fiona) just as present action during *Second Skin* (the birth of a son) *seems* triumphant over past action (the death of a daughter). Though positive eventualities (Meredith's flight, Catherine's recovery) balance out negative ones (Hugh's death, Fiona's disappearance), however, Cyril, no less than Skipper, remains an *impotent* survivor, and so *The Blood Oranges*, no less than *Second Skin*, grants Eros merely an ostensible victory.

Cyril's remark about Catherine and himself being "the two halves of the ancient fruit" infers that opposition may be complementary. "Catherine is the mother-version of Fiona; Fiona is the Aphrodite of Catherine. The two are probably one." [67] Slender Fiona and Hugh complement heavy Catherine and Cyril, the younger couple on one occasion dashing far ahead "long-legged and impetuous," "flaunting their eagerness and similarity of temperament," to await "the slow strollers." And Cyril observes, "How different we were, Fiona and I, and yet how similar." "Different" because in church they approach altars "nearly opposite in color, mood, design"; in nature he reflects the grape arbor and she the lemon grove; and in Illyria his favorite hour, twilight, alternates with hers, dawn. "Similar" because each is "perfectly aware of the other's thoughts" and shares "the same taste and motivation," even competing "for Hugh's life from the first moment."

Union between Cyril and Fiona parallels union between Cyril and Catherine. At one point, he says he lay awake and remembered another condition of "warmth, surprise, pleasure." This was Fiona's marriage bed, where he had also lain awake with a clear mind feeling something had changed after carrying her to the fountain. The change now made logical associations flow and thus Fiona became Catherine sleeping nearby and marriage "the promise of sexless matrimony."

Such complemental relationships pervade *The Blood Oranges*, which treats concord as well as discord. Seen positively, the book resembles a mandala. The mandala, according to Jung, who believes that the unconscious mind considers the quaternion wholer than the triad, symbolizes fourness and God. In *The Blood Oranges*, fourness is expressed by two couples, God by erotic love.

Consequently, Hawkes adopts an older, physiological concept of characterization appropriate to a novel preoccupied with the medieval past. That concept involves the four humours of blood, phlegm, yellow bile, and black bile:

Both physical diseases and mental and moral dispositions ("temperaments") were caused by the condition of the *humours*. Disease resulted from the dominance of some element within a single *humour*, or from a lack of balance or proportion among the *humours* themselves. The *humours* gave off vapors which ascended to the brain. An individual's personal characteristics, physical, mental, and moral, were explained by his "temperament" or the state of his *humours*. The perfect temperament resulted when no one *humour* dominated. The sanguine man has a dominance of blood, is beneficent, joyful, amorous. The choleric man is easily

angered, impatient, obstinate, vengeful. The phlegmatic man is
dull, pale, cowardly. The melancholic man is gluttonous, backward, unenterprising, thoughtful, sentimental, affected.[68]

The humours operate flexibly in Hawkes's modern allegory. Sanguine Cyril, though beneficent, joyful, and amorous, prefers gold to red; choleric Fiona (yellow), though
impatient, seldom manifests anger, obstinacy, vengeful-
ness; phlegmatic Catherine, though dull, appears neither
pale nor cowardly; and melancholic Hugh (black), though
backward, unenterprising, thoughtful, and sentimental, is
not gluttonous or affected.

The fact that these four characters represent the four
humours explains why Hawkes regards Cyril, Fiona, Hugh,
and Catherine as "versions of a single figure . . . the
components, the parts, the inadequate fragments of human
nature." [69] Cyril waits "for the parents to become lovers and
the lovers parents" and asserts, "We are all interchangeable." Conscious that the two couples express one temperament, he says: they "fit together like the shapely pieces of a
perfectly understandable puzzle"; they "constituted the
four major points of the compass"; they comprised a
"four-pointed constellation." They are seen "holding
hands," "bound together," "standing shoulder to shoulder," "climbing . . . in unchanged order." Their clothes,
repeatedly contrasted ("yellow suede coat, white pullover,
blue jacket, and peagreen slacks"), bear "some similarity";
the "characteristic gesture" of each ("Catherine with her
hands at her sides, Hugh clutching his impertinent camera,
Fiona unconsciously holding her breasts . . . I bare-
chested and cigarette in mouth and staring with bland eyes
at a full wineglass lifted high") reveals "an experience,
purpose and continuity."

In addition to the Jungian mandala and the medieval humours, Hawkes's foursome represents the musical quartet, whose properties Aaron Copland has described:

The most usual of all chamber-music combinations is that of the string quartet, composed of two violins, viola and cello. . . . Within its own frame it is an admirably polyphonic medium, by which I mean that it exists in terms of the separate voices of the four instruments. In listening to the string quartet, you must be prepared to listen contrapuntally. [70]

Like Eliot's *Four Quartets, The Blood Oranges* employs such string quartet devices as recurrence with modifications and counterpointing. Hawkes feels that harmony through language communicates love and love expresses life. He calls his novel "lyrically comic" (Interview), and Cyril, whose name is an anagram for "lyric," often refers to "lyricism."

Fiona's voice is strident, Catherine's subdued, Cyril's confidential, Hugh's constricted. Dissonant and childish himself, Hugh, who transforms "our lovely song" into "a shriek," has fathered querulous-sounding children.

He may shatter the quartet's but not the protagonist's equilibrium. In a book full of elaborate vocal-linguistic arrangements, Cyril, the "faithful sex-singer" identified with birds, initiates love by oral persuasion. Catherine is "audible rather than visible" on their first night together, so he must *hear* her mood. Does "We've been married a long time" imply security, resignation, indignation? Does "I'm forty-three" imply self-awareness, diversion, confidence? Does "All right" imply "a troubled or low-pitched acquiescence or even worse a defensive gesture"? As the two trade secrets, Cyril interprets Catherine's "accent." He manipulates his own voice, using "lower, more reassuring registers," giving back words "like low notes on a flute." He contrives a seduction strategy to avoid Catherine's silent children and deaf dog, then leads her toward intimacy "in unspoken accord."

Meanwhile, the simultaneous flirtation between Hugh and Fiona remains unconsummated, for Cyril notes, "I heard nothing more, no sighing, not even the solace of a deliberately noisy kiss." Fiona is also audible rather than visible. The "laughing, preoccupied frosty whisper," "the playful confusion of footsteps," "the silence" suggest "happiness" at first, but later "lyrical sex-play" becomes "girlish grief" when Fiona's "sleepy voices" intones "death or departure."

Through oral persuasion, Cyril converts Catherine to love and life during the present action. Every week he encounters "childish silence," his "patient monologues" notwithstanding. Yet the hope that she will retract "her vow of speechlessness" and "share with me the still music . . . of sexless matrimony" finally is realized as she agrees to be the "muted presence on the other side of my crude bedroom wall." Their symbolic wedding, following Cyril's observation "No music in the way she moved," hinges upon Catherine's regained articulateness ("I never expected to talk to you again").

The parallel courtship of Rosella is conducted *exclusively* along oral lines:

She cooks, she draws water, I spend my time attempting to inflame Rosella with words she does not understand, attempting to surround the ignorant virginity of Rosella's spirit with at least the spoken tones of joy and desire. I have made myself rules: no touching, nothing overt. Only the spoken tones of joy and desire.

Soon Cyril must confess there have been no clandestine trysts despite her need for a physical token of ardor. Although this maiden inherited from Hugh spurns other suitors, little actual communication occurs. The reasons are evident. Cyril's impotence increases when he utters words Rosella finds incomprehensible, while Rosella hardly speaks from "one month to the next." Moreover, she has a monogamous, puritanical bias which the rejection of the village lover, the married fishermen, and the old man demonstrates. Hugh's "last peasant nude" resembles him.

A passage treating a hunchback admirer indicates that even the Mediterranean language may be transformed by love: "And out of all that leathern bulk and deformity of a man who looked like a capped and muzzled bear came a voice that suggested only the softness and clarity of a young girl's voice poured from a shy pitcher." Nevertheless, the native tongue is essentially ugly. It includes two expressions, *croak peonie* and *crespi fagag*, barbaric syllables as unintelligible as the graffiti at the fortress. These expressions contribute much of the abrasive noise connected with southern Europe, both human ("muttered threats," "grunting," "gruff intermittent shouts," "brutal, imperative instructions") and non-human ("obsolete mechanical horn," "archaic heart-shaped stringed instrument," "small rusty pear-shaped iron bells"). Visiting Catherine, Cyril speculates, "Surely the sanctuary was conceived and built by someone who could never vocalize the harsh unimaginative language of this terrain." "Harsh" and "unimaginative" also define Hugh's language because he too represents dissonance.

Countless allusions to "aesthetic" intimate that Cyril, the vocal-linguistic tactician, is a self-conscious artist. Other allusions to literary endowment and technique recall Skipper. Having descended from him, Hawkes's Illyrian narrator develops an elaborate tapestry through recurrent images. The warp is the story, the weaver, the storyteller. A

bright design disclosing "the map of love" results. This
design is graphic and its designer, who compares Fiona's
hands with Leonardo's and analyzes chapel sketches,
dominates it: "I completed the picture"; "you stood in the
upper right or lower left-hand corner"; "my re-entry"; "I
. . . carried my now clamorous companion into a distant
corner." Cyril thus attempts to promote harmony by means
of visual as well as oral strategies.

   Pursuing the same goal, Hawkes provides his narrator
with a formally serene atmosphere. *The Blood Oranges* and
*Second Skin* are pastoral fictions. As the earlier book was
designated "pastoral, but not merely in creating an ideal or
idyllic life," the later book is designated "a pastoral novel"
that welds "gratuitous and coherent" experience (Interview). Skipper and Cyril both refer to the pastoral genre,
Skipper mentioning "our pastoral" and Cyril "the hot pastoral grade." "A pastoral person," Skipper's heir employs
the words "idyl," "idyls," "idyllic." "Idyling." Rightly so, for
*The Blood Oranges* qualifies under the dictionary definition
of pastoral—"a poem, play, or the like, dealing with the life of
shepherds, commonly in a conventional or artificial manner, or with simple rural life generally." [71] Although the
manner may not be conventional and the subject may not be
the life of shepherds, this artificial work does treat rural life.
Hawkes's sophisticated lovers meet a goat-girl on one occasion, a shepherd on another. And, moving among symbolic
animals, objects, people, and plants, Cyril, "the white bull,"
often alludes to symbolic sheep and goats.

   But like *Second Skin*, *The Blood Oranges* also treats
paradise lost. Its epigraph drawn from Ford Maddox
Ford's *The Good Soldier* asks, "Is there then any terrestrial
paradise where, amidst the whispering of the olive-leaves,
people can be with whom they like and have what they like
and take their ease in shadows and in coolness?" The an-

swer is "No" because "even in the most paradisal of the
worlds I've created the roses conceal deadly thorns." [72]
Pastoral successor to *Second Skin,* the equally paradoxical
*Blood Oranges* explores those "barbs . . . hidden
beneath . . . flowers."

Its epigraph comes from *The Good Soldier,* but its landscape from *Twelfth Night* ("a city in Illyria, and the seacoast
near by"). Indeed Shakespeare's play inspired Hawkes's
novel, as "*The Blood Oranges* was in part based on my own
feelings about *Twelfth Night* and I wanted very much to
strive for the ambience, atmosphere, harmony that exist in
the play" (Interview). Hawkes has further explained:

Then suddenly I visualized a fragmented scene of some children
carrying a coffin which contained a dead dog, and being followed
by four adults, which was the begining of *The Blood Oranges.* At
that moment I was quite aware of *Twelfth Night,* that beautiful
whole in which all of our fragmented selves are finally realigned
into the ultimate harmony. In *The Blood Oranges* I wanted to strive
toward precisely that kind of structure. [73]

In *Twelfth Night,* fragmentation (the Duke loves Olivia
who loves Viola [disguised] who loves the Duke) and
realignment (Olivia wins Sebastian, Viola the Duke) lead
toward a quaternion; in *The Blood Oranges,* they generate a
triad (past action) and a dyad (present action). Even
Hawkes's use of Shakespeare's subplot is negative. Cyril, a
latter-day Sir Toby by virtue of his "cakes and ale"
philosophy, tells Hugh that Fiona calls him Malvolio and
"says she loves her Malvolio best." This analogy between
Malvolio and Hugh has considerable importance, for Hugh
acts the churlish, egotistical Puritan too. He is discovered in
"a dark room" by Cyril much as Master Parson is imprisoned "in a dark house" by Sir Toby. Both mad, both are

"Out o' tune" while Shakespearean songs and Hawkesian voices express "the food of love." They play ends harmoniously with Sir Toby virile and Malvolio appeased, but the novel ends disharmoniously with Cyril impotent and Hugh dead.

*The Blood Oranges* was composed "in the tradition of high comedy" to acquire "a sense of harmony and lyric unity" (Interview), yet, instead of arousing thoughtful laughter through exposing human inconsistencies and incongruities, the novel has elicited only solemn reviews. Hawkes, already disappointed over a similar reaction to *Second Skin*, blames his readers: "In *The Blood Oranges* I gather that the concern with adultery is so threatening that again readers simply fail to respond to the entire fiction as comic. The problem is what the reader brings to the novel" (Interview). Curiously enough, if he brings a concept of comedy derived from works like *Twelfth Night*, whose lovers are foolish though innocent and whose main plot treats discord culminating in concord, he will find *The Blood Oranges* essentially non-comic. Its action, which manipulates the modern strategies of "wife-swapping" instead of the traditional devices of disguise and mistaken identity, emphasizes Hugh's death, Fiona's flight, Catherine's illness, and Cyril's impotence. Its principal characters have permanent faults: Hugh's antipathy toward sex, Cyril's toward children. They more nearly resemble the antagonists of *Twelfth Night*'s dark subplot than the protagonists of the comic main plot.

Hawkes nevertheless offers *The Blood Oranges* as "a partial alternative" to *The Lime Twig* and *The Good Soldier*:

But I also had *The Lime Twig* and *The Good Soldier* in mind. I wasn't trying to parody either of those novels, but was trying to create a partial alternative to them. *The Good Soldier* is another fiction in which sexual "extension" results in total destructiveness. By the time of *The Blood Oranges,* I had certainly begun to see other possibilities (Interview).

Destructiveness results from *The Lime Twig* and *The Good Soldier* because *The Lime Twig* concludes with the annihilation of Michael and Margaret and *The Good Soldier* with the suicide of Florence and Edward and the remarriage of Leonora. Twoness anticipating threeness is "a partial alternative" to nothingness or oneness.

 *The Blood Oranges* owes *The Good Soldier* even more than it does *Twelfth Night.* For Hawkes, this "comic and terrifying" novel employs an irony that conveys his own central paradox: "both a sense of the ideal and a devastating impression of the impossibility of human relationships" (Interview). These relationships involve mature men and women. "When we all first met" in *The Good Soldier,* Edward was thirty-three, Leonora thirty-one, Dowell thirty-six, and Florence thirty. "At the height of our season" in *The Blood Oranges,* "Fiona and Hugh were almost forty," Catherine "several years" older, and Cyril "two or three long leaps beyond middle age." Dowell becomes Hugh, Florence Fiona, Edward Cyril, Leonora Catherine. But Ford's quaternion, which matches a puritanical male (Dowell) and a promiscuous female (Florence) and a promiscuous male (Edward) and a puritanical female (Leonora) through marriage and then rematches the promiscuous pair through adultery and the puritanical pair through conspiracy, is reversed by Hawkes. His promiscuous and puritanical couples are wed before promiscuous Cyril joins puritanical Catherine and puritanical Hugh promiscuous Fiona. He reverses their destinies too. Whereas *The Good Soldier* has puritanical Dowell-Leonora surviving promiscuous Edward-Florence, *The Blood Oranges* has promiscuous

Cyril-Fiona surviving puritanical Hugh. He experiences the Edward-Florence heart condition and suicide during Hawkes's partial alternative.

The first-person narrator is inverted. Naive Dowell, who says about the past, "I had never the remotest glimpse, not the shadow of a suspicion that there was anything wrong," and about the present, "I know nothing—nothing in the world—of the hearts of men," receives information from fundamentally unreliable second-hand accounts, but shrewd Cyril, who takes pride in "my memory, my self-understanding, my ability to expose the logic sewn into the seams of almost all of our precious sequences of love and friendships," gets it from basically reliable first-hand observations. One functions as diarist, the other as artist. Clumsy Dowell admits, "I have, I am aware, told this story in a very rambling way so that it may be difficult for anyone to find his path through what may be a sort of maze," while clever Cyril points out "the true artistic nature of our design," "the aesthetic pattern I had in mind."

At the same time the two narrators resemble one another. Impotent, self-conscious storytellers, they both empathize with their alter egos, when, for example, Dowell confesses, "I can't conceal from myself the fact that I loved Edward Ashburnham—and that I love him because he was just myself. . . . He seems to me like a large elder brother," [74] or when Cyril confesses, "I was Hugh's accomplice. In all my strength and weight I was not so very different from Hugh after all."

Actually, Cyril and Hugh, though "polar opposites," are "versions of a single figure":

Cyril is pure, Hugh is a Puritan; Cyril to me is not a libertine but simply a God-like man with infinite capacities for love. Cyril is a modest but literal lover. Hugh is an idealist. And Hugh's idealism is a totally destructive quality. Cyril is a practitioner of Hugh's idealism, is able to love with the strength and purity that is in fact Hugh's ideal. Hugh's ideal, however, keeps him from loving at all. . . . I think that for me those characters are indeed polar opposites, versions of a single figure; they are both artists. . . . Cyril is probably just as self-destructive as Hugh. Hugh in his death is at least probably as much the visionary as Cyril is.[75]

As versions of a single figure, Cyril supports Hugh during the fortress episode, telling him, "Don't pay any attention to them," and sensing that he, too, "had sought [the chastity belt] and found it and inflicted it on all four of us." Clothing imagery confirms their similarity. Although Hugh "was black while I was gold," Cyril, who later suffers from Hugh's insomnia and impotence, will acquire a "shabby black coat and vest and trousers." Hugh, after succumbing to Fiona, borrows Cyril's "red-and-white striped cotton shirt." *The Blood Oranges,* then, is more than an allegory externalizing the conflict between Eros and Thanatos through oppositional figures. It is also a realistic-psychological study that places the struggle *within* these figures. On the one hand, Cyril and Hugh represent "the two sides of Skipper"; on the other, each of them incorporates both sides. The narrator of *The Blood Oranges,* like the narrator of *Second Skin,* has inherited "those little black seeds of death."

But unlike *Second Skin,* which focuses on an individual, *The Blood Oranges* treats a group. White, Hugh's only color besides black and blue, is appropriate in the quaternary context because "black-and-white" defines the way Cyril's stony antagonist thinks. His "disease," produced by "the dominance of some element within a single *humour,*" causes his death; and the resulting "lack of balance or proportion among the *humours* themselves" destroys the quartet.

*The Blood Oranges* is paradoxical, however. The harmony which disappears with Fiona's departure, Catherine's illness, and Cyril's impotence may eventually be restored through Fiona's return and Cyril's "sexless matrimony," as no one humour controls these characters to the extent that black bile controls Hugh. The paradoxical nature of the novel is thus compounded; if Eros is to triumph, that triumph will occur in the future. Meanwhile, Thanatos prevails.

# Postscript

A direct outgrowth of *The Blood Oranges* and *Second Skin,* Hawkes's most recent novel, *Death, Sleep & the Traveler* (1974), published too late for extended discussion here, confirms previously established patterns.

Its narrator is yet another corpulent, middle-aged Aryan survivor who presents a dramatic monologue or explanation to unseen auditor-judges. That the explanation bears confessional overtones becomes clear from the concluding rationalization, "I am not guilty." This refers to his entire experience as well as to the murder of which he has been accused and acquitted.

All those involved with Allert except Ariane challenge his self-proclaimed innocence. But the issue of vitality seems more important than the issue of guilt. Allert's wife, Ursula, says that he lacks emotional response, while her lover, Peter, says that he exists in a coma. And, indeed, the narrator admits finding everything, himself included, unreal. His Dutch name as "repository for the English word 'alert'" is an ironic way to designate a traveler who personifies Sleep and Death.

152

Allert dreams instead of living. Childless and hostile toward children, he experiences recurrent nightmares and meditations about his own unhappy childhood. The details are few and fuzzy, yet the reader understands that the narrator was abandoned by his mother through death and that somehow her abandonment made him psychologically impotent and physically passive. This familio-environmental circumstance determines Allert's subsequent attitudes and behavior. A libertine collector of pornography, he chooses disloyal women whose infidelities he tolerates, then resents. Ursula and Ariane epitomize these women, for they play the female roles in parallel *ménage à trois* situations.

The conflict between Eros and Thanatos is absent from *Death, Sleep & the Traveler*. There Allert, connecting the two since infancy and even marrying after a funeral, symbolizes both, not as antithetical but synonymous forces.

Hawkes dramatizes Allert's predicament by familiar means. Several unnumbered, untitled sections juxtapose distant past (childhood), past (involvement with Ursula-Peter, with Ariane-Olaf), and present (departure of Ursula) to show the first shaping the second and the second the third. Concomitant juxtapositions among four major settings—Allert's village, Allert's house, Peter's house, and the ship—treat the three periods, giving temporal and spatial phenomena a synchronistic effect. The past or dominant period alternates between two "mythic" landscapes, one frigid—"this small country of ours"—and one tropical—the tainted "Paradise Isles." Iterative imagery is also significant. For example, sex and death are frequently conveyed through allusions to animals (bats, goats, duck, octopus) and physical defects (rashes, heart attack, scar, sunburn). Allert's rash, "At first a few isolated splotchy areas of pebbled crimson," becomes "a broad red welted ring completely encircling the little untouched island of the navel."

Unlike Skipper, who finds a new family, and Cyril, who seduces a new companion, Allert, having lost mother, wife, mistress, and friend, represents Hawkes's only futureless survivor. His will be the fate of the living dead to "simply think and dream, think and dream."

# Interview

John Hawkes was born on August 17, 1925, in Stamford, Connecticut, and spent his childhood and adolescence in Old Greenwich, Connecticut, New York City, Juneau, Alaska, and Poughkeepsie and Pawling, New York. During World War II, he was an American Field Service ambulance driver in Italy and Germany. In 1949, he was graduated from Harvard, where he had studied creative writing under Albert J. Guerard, and where he subsequently taught. Hawkes, who joined the staff of Brown University as an English professor during 1958, has been special guest at the Aspen Institute for Humanistic Studies, director of an experimental writing project at Stanford University, member of the Panel on Educational Innovation (Washington, D.C.), and Visiting Distinguished Professor of Creative Writing at the City College of New York. Awards given him include a Guggenheim Fellowship, 1962; a National Institute of Arts and Letters Grant in Fiction, 1962; a Ford Foundation Fellowship to spend 1964–65 with the Actor's Workshop of San Francisco; and a

Rockefeller Foundation Fellowship to travel and write in Europe during 1967–68.

The following interview, scheduled for publication in modified form by *The Paris Review*, Fall, 1975, transpired on November 8, 1971. It appears here with the permission of Mr. Hawkes and *The Paris Review*. Throughout the text, K stands for Kuehl and H for Hawkes.

K: You stopped writing poetry about the time you started writing fiction.

H: That's right.

K: How could you write a book like *The Cannibal* just after having written what I take to be rather romantic, rather conventional verse?

H: Well, I don't really know. The war intervened and the war was a kind of shocking acting-out of internal nightmare, as if all of our nightmares had become literally real. After the war I turned to prose quite by accident because my wife gave me a novel to read. I didn't like the novel and thought I could do better and began to write with extreme detachment.

K: Weren't you once going to write a biography of Nathanael West?

H: Yes, but I didn't go through with it. I wanted to and I tried, but finally critical-biographical writing was simply not what I was interested in and I wasn't able to do it. I am still very much interested in West. He's one of the few contemporary writers I feel close to. I wrote an essay on Flannery O'Connor called "Flannery O'Connor's Devil" that compares her work with West's.

K: How do such detached writers use autobiographical material as opposed, say, to Thomas Wolfe?

H: I wouldn't want to talk about Flannery O'Connor biographically. She must have been using some materials from the world around her, perhaps her own illness, but I think her imagination was so pure and secure that she was doing what we all want to do, which is to create our own worlds in our own voice. She was probably quite untroubled by autobiographical intrusions. West's writing and life are similarly unrelated. I think he used certain deep impulses and fears that were his own but was able to exploit them so fully and so richly that you would actually find very little autobiographical connection. The kind of life material that interested me in West was, for instance, his swimming pool in Pennsylvania. He wanted very much to have the pool. He was living in California at the time and he kept hearing that his swimming pool was constantly draining and going dry. He wrote innumerable letters about that abortive pool. I understand that he was a bad hunter, but still liked to hunt. There is an anecdote Josephine Herbst told about West hunting in his business suit in her biographical fiction, *Hunter of Doves*. Well, incongruity, a mixture of idealism, and comic ruthlessness—these apparently in some sense were in his life; but the work, to me, stands apart and I would say that my own writing is similarly separate from my life. It is not defined by biographical connections.

к: That's interesting because several people have commented on the normality of your environment and behavior and you've insisted that you're a conventional man.

н: True.

к: And yet your fiction disturbs conventional people.

н: I'm glad it does. Insofar as I think of it in terms of intention, I want my fiction to destroy conventional morality and conventional attitudes. That's part of its purpose —to challenge us in every way possible in order to cause us to know ourselves better and to live with more compassion.

к: Would you say that to some extent your fiction is

aimed at yourself, at the values you inherited or grew up with?

H: I find paradox everywhere. On the one hand, my fiction depends on a kind of cold, detached, authoritarian stance which I could think of as puritanical, but insofar as the fiction is personal it is so only in the sense that I'm interested in destroying puritanism, overcoming puritanical morality. The very subject I'm trying to overcome provides the emotional stance necessary to do the writing in the first place. But the fiction isn't aimed at myself. I don't think of myself when I'm trying to write and I'm not concerned with my own life or my own interests. I'm simply trying to create a new world, a new landscape in order to use the language in some newly necessary way.

K: What about the immediate paradox of living a pattern of life that elsewhere you attack?

H: Well, if I appear to live conventionally I don't suppose that means that I am conventional. In actual relationships with other people, I hope I'm not predictable or conventional. In thinking and talking I try to be disruptive and honest. I try to get to the serious and difficult questions, and my life is essentially a matter of being ruthless in terms of certain ideas but generally compassionate. Idealism and innocence lie behind everything that I write and I spend my time trying to be as clear and direct and truthful with other people as possible. It is difficult to achieve a kind of real human presence when you are actually relating to others humanly and poetically and attempting to overcome our conventional stances, our various repressions, inhibitions.

K: So those who take you negatively are missing the very point?

H: It would be absurd to take my fiction as negative. It is quite the opposite.

к: Would you comment on whatever formal religious background you have?

н: I was brought up as an Episcopalian. But that word has no meaning to me except that it immediately prompts me to a feeling of inner resistance. I remember playing a trumpet in a church in Alaska. I remember sitting in a gloomy church—perhaps a Sunday school—in New York City. I was born in Connecticut, but we lived in New York for awhile when I was quite young. I remember other children in that group talking about kicking a baby around the street in a gunny sack. But I can't account for my puritanism.

к: A strong element of Christian allegory runs through your works.

н: I want to deny it.

к: Could I cite a scene for you?

н: Sure.

к: In *Second Skin* Skipper, who is the Catholic chaplain's acolyte, the keeper of the cross, confronts Tremlow, who is repeatedly called "devil."

н: Right.

к: During this scene, Tremlow and the other mutineers seem to "gang-bang" Skipper in the lifeboat.

н: Tremlow does rape Skipper, and Skipper is indeed saved by the Catholic chaplain.

к: You refer to Skipper as Jonah. What would you say about that?

н: Well, I knew about the garden of Gethsemane from a colleague at Brown when I was trying to teach tragedy and was working with *Hamlet*. I had taught only writing at Harvard before that moment and my charitable friend helped me with the Christian symbolism in *Hamlet*. Like Christ, Hamlet prepares for his impending death, and when I was writing *Second Skin* that scene came to mind. You remember

Skipper lies in his bunk before going up to the pilothouse, where Tremlow appears with the ax, in a state of knowing that some dread event is to occur, and he is prepared to be sacrificed to it. I thought of that whole moment as comic and poignant. It was a way of dramatizing the emotional quality of the event and of using deeply serious biblical ideas as a starting place for comedy. But I don't know the Bible; I'm not widely read. I didn't really have any formal religious experiences in my childhood or past. It's paradoxical that someone who knows as little about religious experience and about the Bible as I do nonetheless uses some of these materials.

к: You also draw on pagan myths and rituals.

н: Can you give me an example?

к: Your parody or travesty of the Osiris myth in *The Beetle Leg*.

н: I'm not familiar with the Osiris myth. I did some reading in Campbell's *Hero of a Thousand Faces* when I was revising *The Lime Twig*.

к: Had you read *The Golden Bough*?

н: I've never read *The Golden Bough*. I don't know where I became acquainted with ritual and myth. I suppose I picked them up along the way with Christianity.

к: At any rate, you do seem to have a rather negative view of formal religion, especially Protestantism.

н: I do.

к: Is this involved in some profound way with sex or sexual inhibition, a kind of perverse channeling off of sexual impulses?

н: I'm now consciously opposed to religion. I think that religion does indeed depend on repression, on the lawful arranging of one's life, and also offers consolations that let us off the hook. I do not believe in any kind of god or any kind of afterlife, obviously. It seems to me necessary to live by creating our own contexts within the constant knowledge of the imminence of annihilation.

K: Although one finds no god in your fiction, many of your characters are identified with Christ—for example, Ernst in *The Cannibal*.

H: But that's a negative association, isn't it? When Ernst is fanatically involved with the little carvings of Christ, he is approaching his own death in an absurd way.

K: Michael Banks stops the Golden Bowl in the posture of the cruciform. A dove flies up and Banks is wearing a rose.

H: Well, all of the Christian symbolism at the end of *The Lime Twig* was pointed out to me by a graduate student at Brown. I wasn't that aware of it. The name of the race, the Golden Bowl, simply came from the title of Henry James's novel. I didn't know where James got the title.

K: You hadn't read Ecclesiastes?

H: No. The student turned to Ecclesiastes and began to read passages from it, including the reference to the great cloud that will rise up with the destruction of the Golden Bowl. Of course, there is an enormous cloud that rises when Michael Banks destroys the race. It seems to me that such Christian symbolism was used unconsciously or at best semi-consciously; but more important, it is the kind of ritualizing or symbolizing that I'm trying to escape.

K: Is that so?

H: Yes, trying to destroy. In *Second Skin* Skipper gives away the golden cross. He doesn't need the cross anymore. He is his own god. He becomes god, which expresses my attitude as well. We ourselves are the source of everything, the indignities as well as the potentials for beauty, serenity, grace, and so on.

K: I detect a lot of Satans and Antichrists in your books. Are you aware of these?

H: When I was giving one of my first readings, a student asked me if I thought I was the Devil. It was a moment of genuine pleasure. But the satanic stance is merely another way of trying to achieve authoritarian detachment, a kind of ruthlessness in the making of fiction. One way of dramatizing and sustaining such detachment is through attacking sacred figures or sacred institutions.

K: You do seem to sympathize with first-person narrators like Zizendorf who appear satanic.

H: Reversed sympathy seems essential to the novelistic or fictional experience. If the point is to discover true compassion, true sympathy, then clearly the task is to sympathize with what we ordinarily take to be truly repulsive in life—hence identification with the so-called criminal or rebellious mentality. I think of the act of writing as an act of rebellion because it is so single and it dares to presume to create the world. I enjoy a sense of violation, a criminal resistance to safety, to the security provided by laws or systems. I'm trying to find the essential human experiences when we are unhinged or alienated from familiar, secure life.

K: In connection with first-person narrators, you once said that you preferred William Hencher to Sidney Slyter. What is there about Slyter that you dislike so much?

H: The Sidney Slyter sections of *The Lime Twig* were written last. James Laughlin, the publisher of New Directions, had suggested that perhaps the novel would benefit by a gloss in the manner of "The Ancient Mariner." I liked the idea, so I tried to parody both the gloss—the commentary on the fiction which Sidney Slyter offers—and the journalist's mind. Sidney Slyter does seem to me to be the only character in my fiction that might approach a genuinely damned state. I don't believe in damnation, as I've said, but within the context of conventional Christianity he is incapable of love, incapable of sympathy, incapable of identifying with anyone, and exists purely as a kind of mechanism of curiosity. To me, he would be closest to the "publishing scoundrel" in *The Aspern Papers,* somebody whose impulses are purely exploitative. I think of him as inhuman. On the other hand, he is funny and, I suppose, he too has his poignancies in that he begins to participate a little in the dream and loses the girl. I thought of him as a comic device. Hencher, on the other hand, is filled with human sensibility. He's trying to love, trying to become involved in sexual experience, even if it is only masturbatory. He is very much alive. He suffers nightmare; he suffers psychic sexual loss. He was the bridge between the war and the postwar world in *The Lime Twig,* and as a deprived man fixated on his dead mother he contains all of the liabilities of life and the struggle to exist. So I'm very sympathetic to Hencher.

к: Hencher participates in the pattern of incest which I find in your work.

н: I hadn't thought much about incest. If the subject came up in an audience, I would no doubt argue for incest out of perversity, but, mind you, surface perversity in me always has at its root much deeper, serious concerns for human emotions. But incest doesn't mean as much to me as it did, say, to Faulkner.

к: Was Hencher your first serious effort to use a first-person narrator?

н: Yes. The first-person narrator of *The Cannibal* was, in a sense, merely mechanical. *The Owl* was written in the first person as an effort to rewrite *The Cannibal.* But the narrator of *The Owl* emerged as a godlike voice rather than the articulated personality of a genuinely created character. With Hencher I knew I was giving voice to an individualized character. With Hencher suddenly the first-person method became real and possible for me and he is the source of Skipper in *Second Skin* who is, in turn, the source of Cyril in *The Blood Oranges*. I think that from narrator to narrator there is a kind of rarefying of their roles and of their rhetoric.

ᴋ: Would you say there is also increasing complexity in terms of characterization? Skipper is an extremely complex figure.

ʜ: I don't know whether Cyril is. Cyril may not be as complexly rendered a character as Skipper.

ᴋ: I've thought of Cyril and Hugh as somehow representing the two sides of Skipper.

ʜ: Fine. They dramatize the polarity of what we have been talking about in the light of religious experience and authorial impulse. On the one hand, I am darkly committed to the puritan ethic. On the other, I detest it and want to destroy it. And in crude terms Cyril and Hugh represent that polarity. All this probably suggests a vestige of the romantic temperament. But, of course, I think I have a kind of clarity and concern with absurdity that mitigates against romantic impulse.

ᴋ: Are your satanic first-person narrators an attempt to purge the author and the reader?

ʜ: I no longer believe in the necessity of purgation or expiation. Exposure, facing, knowing, experiencing the worst as well as best of our inner impulses—these are the things that I'm concerned with.

ᴋ: You once referred to fishing for yourself.

ʜ: I said that "the author is his own best angleworm and the sharper the barb with which he fishes himself out of the darkness the better." This, to me, is another paradoxical statement in that when I think of the writer exploiting himself or his own psychic life I'm thinking impersonally. I mean that the writer who exploits his own psychic life reveals the inner lives of us all, the inner chaos, the negative aspects of the personality in general. I'm appalled at violence, opposed to pain, terrified of actual destructiveness. Obviously, the eating of the child in *The Cannibal* is an agony. It isn't that I'm advocating that we live by acts of violence; I, myself, don't want to live the nightmare. It's just that our deepest inner lives are largely organized around such impulses, which need to be exposed and understood and used. Even appreciated.

к: You have spoken of the detectives in *The Lime Twig* as somehow representing the author. Were you serious?

н: Partly. But you were making a connection between the first-person narrator and diabolical intelligence.

к: Even what you have called "sadistic impulses."

н: But I don't necessarily make any connection between first-person narrators and the sadistic mentality or the authoritarian stand of the writer.

к: Is that a change?

н: Well, the narrator of *The Owl* is a dictator, a fascist leader, but Hencher is not diabolical or satanic. Nor is Skipper, nor is Cyril.

к: How about Larry?

н: Larry is a diabolical character. My sympathies are all with Larry.

к: Why?

н: In "real" life, the world's hostility would be leveled against him. He's the superb (though parodied) outcast working or trying to live against the greatest odds. He's exerting himself and his own loneliness to attempt to create a world. He merely appears to be the source of evil in *The Lime Twig*.

к: Freud says there is a struggle in human beings between the Death-Force or aggression and the Life-Force or Eros, and in the allegorical framework of your books—for

example, *Second Skin*—these forces seem to be in conflict.
Are they innate?

H: I suppose they are culturally created. I'm not much
interested in their sources. It's true that all of my fiction
does depend on the conflict between sexual or life possibility and drives toward destruction and death. A kind of
death-ridden fiction, I suppose, but much of the negative
sexual material—what Albert Guerard called the landscape
of sexual apathy—is a metaphor of the destructiveness of
the forces working against us and therefore of our inability
to love. In other words, I don't think that I'm simply writing
about castration, say. When we talk about the inner psychic
life, certainly I'm trying to deal with childhood fears, fears
of being devoured, overwhelmed, punished, and also, I
suppose, desires to exert oneself toward freedom.

K: Would you say that Michael Banks's act in *The Lime
Twig* is in act of love against death?

H: Yes, it's an act of retribution, but now I'm not at all
convinced that that retribution was necessary or justified. I
remember being in a class when a student, a young girl,
said, "Why can't Michael Banks simply know that series of
women and survive, go on living in a perfectly normal
way?" and I was taken aback by the question. In the larger
sense, I still believe that his pursuit of the dream ending in
destruction is one valid way of looking at life. Pedestrian
minds (and they're the most numerous) are always out to
destroy the dreams or the dreamer, destroy the effort to
pursue some ideal. But, on the other hand, I no longer
believe myself, inwardly, that we are indeed so limited. In
other words, I now want to challenge concepts like guilt,
retribution, atonement, etc., since I no longer believe that
the pursuit of the dream, say, in sexual terms—such as
Cyril's efforts to destroy monogamy—is necessarily evil or
destructive.

K: "Evil" is a word you've called "pure."

H: For me evil was once a power. Now it's a powerful metaphor. I'm so convinced that we ourselves do all the "creating" that I can't believe in any great satanic force existing outside of us or pursuing us from some dark past. The concept of world as prison needs to be destroyed. (The real prisons need destroying too.) But it's quite possible to create moments of idyllic life.

K: I detect an increasing tendency to make your fiction more dramatic. Does this have anything to do with the plays you wrote in the mid-sixties?

H: I don't think so. I didn't write plays until after *Second Skin.* But perhaps the writing of dialogue relates to the plays; I suppose there is an increasing use of dialogue in *The Blood Oranges.* At any rate, the most interesting of the plays is *The Questions,* and that was an effort to see how much narrative I could get into drama, not the other way around.

K: I see the fiction up to *The Blood Oranges* as being rather deterministic, but in this latest novel you don't put much emphasis on the personal past.

H: I deliberately omitted the past lives of the characters.

K: Would you say that's a shift in attitude toward life?

H: It's a shift in attitude toward fiction.

K: We don't need to know Cyril's background?

H: I wanted to create characters in total purity and to deny myself the novelistic easiness of past lives to draw on. It's easier to sustain fiction with flashbacks, with a kind of explanatory reconstruction of past lives. All this adds more possibilities for drama, etc. I wanted none of it. I was trying to make *The Blood Oranges* pure for the sake of comedy, and I wanted to struggle with the characters without letting the past intrude. *The Cannibal,* of course, does not rely on any information about the past lives of its characters.

к: Stella . . . .

н: That's true.

к: And Jutta . . . .

н: Okay. *The Lime Twig,* on the other hand, reveals very little about the past lives of Michael or Margaret. They're the innocent figures from nowhere cast down onto the illusionary stage. They're closer to the characters in *The Blood Oranges.*

к: I felt that you were making an effort to give your characters a choice in *The Lime Twig* and that this effort was made again in *Second Skin* and *The Blood Oranges.*

н: Banks chooses to die. Skipper manages to survive. Cyril is impotent while telling his story. Actually, the idea of choice had little to do with the writing of these novels.

к: A perceptive reader told me that the absence of a scene between Fiona and Cyril before she departs with the children makes her final view of him unclear.

н: We last see Fiona and Cyril together over Hugh's dead body, and to me her attitude toward Cyril is clear enough. Fiona is likely to return, but the ending of *The Blood Oranges* hinges on the idea of life starting over for Catherine and Cyril. The boat scene represents their wedding. Some reviewers of *The Blood Oranges* have criticized Cyril for being a manipulator, as exerting inhuman control over the relationship between all four characters. I don't think the novel supports this limited idea. At any rate, the reviewers have been repelled by Cyril's power, but have failed to point out his impotence (which, incidentally, is the result of Hugh's actually gratuitous death).

н: You don't see Cyril as having caused it?

н: He didn't cause Hugh's death at all. Hugh dies because his solipsized sexual impulses and his puritanism were finally too strong even for Fiona. In other words, the action of the novel is Hugh's resistance to Fiona, which climaxes in his forcing the chastity belt upon Catherine, which in turn precipitates Cyril's major effort to convince Hugh to accept Fiona's love. But after the argument in the grape arbor, which Cyril wins, there follows a long idyllic period in which the four characters are actually intermingling their loves, as the jacket says. What's left out is that all this time, while Hugh is finally knowing Fiona sexually, he has nonetheless still been experiencing his own inner solipsized sexual life through his photographs and that dangling rope.

κ: He continues to masturbate, doesn't he?

н: The point is that after he becomes Fiona's lover he is still at the mercy of his inner and thoroughly isolated sexual life. Hugh doesn't mean to kill himself. He means to undergo a partial hanging in order to experience sexual release, but he slips and thus accidentally dies. I meant the death of Hugh in a sense to trick the reader into thinking of it as a moral judgment on the multiple relationships—but to me it is not. Hugh's death is thoroughly absurd. Paradoxically, Cyril's mind gives rise to sensuality; his comic rationalism ends in lyricism. In *The Blood Oranges,* which is a pastoral novel, experience is viewed as both gratuitous and coherent.

κ: Both Skipper and Cyril survive. Is your notion of survival similar to what Faulkner thinks of as "endure"?

н: Not at all. I don't believe in the "old verities."

κ: It is a positive value, though, in your world, simply to survive?

н: To keep living is the point.

κ: Morally, amorally, however?

н: Any way at all. Faulkner's "enduring" posits a moral courage, a moral stance that is unfamiliar to me. To me, the first values are found in the most demeaned kinds of life. I don't think of life as something to be endured. It's something to be created and lived.

K: As I read your fiction, children are victims generally killed in the course of the action.

H: That's true.

K: Is Meredith of *The Blood Oranges* different from previous children?

H: Well, up to Meredith, all of the children in some way or another are prefigurations of the author. In a sense, the children can be taken as authorial innocence, purity, and are the victims of our corrupt conventional, apparently moral, but actually destructive world. However, Pixie in *Second Skin* is no longer such a representation. She is simply a small difficult particle of life, messy with strawberry jam, that Skipper manages to embrace. She's as free of morality as the little twin girls in *The Blood Oranges*. Meredith, on the other hand, condemns what she thinks of as the adulterous, destructive love of her parents and Fiona and Cyril. She's exemplary of conventional hostility towards law-breaking. She threatens our attitudes toward Cyril, she makes us doubt him or question him at certain moments, she elicits his sadism. She's conscience and comic foil combined. Cyril's incapacity, it seems to me, is precisely to be unable to love children.

K: One of the most disturbing things in your fiction is the facility with which children are corrupted. I'm thinking now of Adeppi in *The Goose on the Grave*. Having been exposed to evil, he fondles an older woman and becomes indirectly responsible for her blind husband's death.

H: I don't remember *The Goose on the Grave*. But at least my child characters are often destroyed if not corrupted.

K: You also use childlike adults—for instance, Margaret and Michael of *The Lime Twig*.

H: These characters simply have to do with my preoc-cupation with innocence (which shouldn't preclude sexual experience). I was trying to articulate that idea and make it more convincing in *The Blood Oranges*, in which a few adult characters are freed of the question of guilt in their sexual lives. Cyril insists that they are all pure, all innocent, no matter what they are doing—which is my own view.

K: Did you intend his name to be an anagram for "lyric"?

H: No. A *Look* magazine reviewer assigned symbolic meanings to the names of the characters in *The Blood Oranges*, and then condemned the novel for being overtly symbolic. But it's a silly idea, and his not mine. The names of my characters have no special intended meaning or significance.

K: Is your book a parody of *Twelfth Night*?

H: To some extent. *The Blood Oranges* was in part based on my own feelings about *Twelfth Night*, and I wanted very much to strive for the ambience, atmosphere, harmony that exist in the play. But I also had *The Lime Twig* and *The Good Soldier* in mind. I wasn't trying to parody either of those novels, but was trying to create a partial alternative to them. *The Good Soldier* is another fiction in which sexual "exten-sion" results in total destructiveness. By the time of *The Blood Oranges*, I had certainly begun to see other pos-sibilities.

K: When you were writing parody consciously, as you were in *The Lime Twig*, was it mostly a matter of literary form or attitude or both?

H: Both. I was attacking cheapness of mind and trying to find a new structure for my language and thematic con-cerns.

K: You've spoken frequently about the failure of read-ers to consider you a comic novelist. Do you miss a comic reaction in the reviews of *The Blood Oranges*?

H: I can't think of a review that's discussed *The Blood Oranges* as comic; whereas I hoped most of all to write this novel in the tradition of high comedy.

K: How would you explain the discrepancy between your own vision and the reaction even intelligent readers have?

H: Well, at least up until *The Blood Oranges,* people have been so overwhelmed by the terror and destructiveness of the life created in my fictions that the comedy has apparently not been evident. With *Second Skin* I was determined to write a comic novel, and I think more readers took it as comedy, though students still appear to care more about the horror than the comic elements of *Second Skin.* In *The Blood Oranges,* I gather that the concern with adultery is so threatening that again readers simply fail to respond to the entire fiction as comic. The problem is what the reader brings to the novel.

K: When I look at *Second Skin* as an ironic novel, the comedy becomes very clear to me.

H: Yes.

K: Comedy in *The Aspern Papers* also depends upon a discrepancy between the narrator's view of the events and the author's.

H: I don't think there's anything humorous or comic about *The Aspern Papers.* It seems to me that the "publishing scoundrel" is at times light-hearted, confident, but is always a cruel and despicable fool. Through the two women—the old woman and her daughter—the reader is constantly made aware of the vastness of the narrator's insensitivity. But *The Good Soldier* is both comic and terrifying. Ford is using irony to produce both a sense of the ideal and a devastating impression of the impossibility of human relationships. *The Blood Oranges* is more lyrically comic than either *The Aspern Papers* or *The Good Soldier.*

κ: You have called comedy "a saving grace." What did you mean?

H: I suppose that in one sense comedy is a form of action in which brutality does not reach its ultimate destructiveness; the victim is not totally punished or destroyed. It would seem to me that the highest forms of comedy may not produce laughter—I mean they're coming up to the edge of laughter and then giving us a kind of light. High comedy simply produces a sense of harmony and lyric unity. I find the subject hard to talk about.

κ: I remember a disturbing scene in *The Beetle Leg* between Cap Leech and the Indian girl during which rape is suggested through a dental operation. Would that be a good example of comedy in your work?

H: In that scene comedy is simply being used to dislodge ordinary expectation so that the horror of the moment has to be perceived in a more complex way. Here comedy is also achieving the detachment necessary to write the scene in the first place. I think we could find richer examples. The scene on the little boat when Skipper sees Captain Red taking his daughter, Cassandra, is highly farcical and there comedy points up the extent of the poignancy of Skipper's reaction to seeing his own daughter in a sexual experience which he himself actually would have wanted to participate in. He's very possessive of his daughter.

κ: He courts her, as I recall, throughout the novel.

H: He does, and that's one of his liabilities. The extent to which he is unaware of his powerful relationship to his daughter is one way we could think of Skipper as an imperceptive narrator. But the comedy in that particular scene also dramatizes Skipper's perseverance. He not only has to suffer watching his daughter, but he's hit on the head by a tire iron. The comedy is used to dramatize both his deter-

mination and his ineffectualness and to make us compassionate to this maimed hero.

K: Is comedy usually double-edged in your writing?

H: Probably. Ironically, it's a child who is hitting Skipper on the head with a tire iron while the one-handed man,
Jomo, is behaving toward Skipper so as to ensure that
Skipper will become seasick. The collusion between Jomo
and the little boy in so grotesque a fashion points up
Skipper's courage or power even in the face of his ineffectual nature. The grotesque victimizing of Skipper while
Cassandra is undergoing a sexual experience also points up
the beauty that's being destroyed or lost for Skipper at that
moment—when, for instance, he sees her pale blue virgin
kerchief sailing off on the wind.

K: As "a saving grace," would you say that comedy has
to do with perception leading toward compassion and un-
derstanding?

H: I suppose it has to do with the multiplicity of experience or with illusion or the fact that any given action may be
much more complex than we would ordinarily think. Comedy involves surprise, and total surprise would have to do
with the vitality of life, the potential for life in a human
being. For example: in *The Blood Oranges*, at the moment on
the beach when Hugh sits on his wife's haunch and paws
her breast, Cyril is conscious of the sexual rapport between
himself and Catherine, is conscious of Catherine's humilia-
tion, is conscious of Hugh being a kind of crude father as he
helps the little child to relieve itself. All of this gives us a
mixture of agony and idealism simultaneously. The difference between Hugh's insensitivity and Cyril's quiet, interior, passionate concern for Catherine's life elevates what
is really no more than a look in the eye and a touch of hands;
so that, in this moment, domesticity becomes a grotesque
travesty harboring genuine love. And then the scene is

disrupted by the appearance of a goat which Cyril has imagined and which turns out to be real. The product of his imagination becomes actual, so that the reader is poised between what is and what isn't and is always perceiving some kind of harmonious, desirable human relationship.

к: Is this the kind of comedy you see in the picaresque tradition?

н: If you're made to laugh at a dismembered body, you experience the horror of dismembering in a different way from simply being confronted and repelled by the stark shock of dismemberment. If part of the purpose of the picaresque is to make us aware of ourselves as possible dismemberers or possible victims, it's clear that we need to experience drastic shifts in what we perceive—hence, the comedy. Comedy violates normal expectations, and it also ameliorates pain through laughter. No doubt laughter is sometimes sadistic and victimizing. In one sense, to laugh at a man may be as great a crime as killing him. Perhaps a worse crime. But at least through laughter there is release, vilification, possible purification, and, finally, identification with the victim.

к: Would this tone explain the re-emergence of the picaresque, with which you have been associated?

н: The only reason I would resist being put in that tradition is because I think my work is unique and because it's so poetically rich. My fiction is probably closer to the attitudes of picaresque fiction than much of what is being written by so-called black humorists, which, after all, is a very surface kind of comedy in which the pain or the true grace of the comic situation is really not so evident. Black humorists, as I would think of them in America today, are very often topical, surface writers.

к: Who do you like among contemporary American novelists?

H: I'd prefer not to talk about who I like. I greatly admire Flannery O'Connor and, of course, Nathanael West. *Nightwood* is a great short novel which I admire enormously. I'm not one of those still trying to minimize Faulkner after the fact. I admire Faulkner as I do Nabokov. John Barth may be our new (of course jocular) Melville.

K: How about William Gaddis?

H: I haven't read him, I'm sorry to say.

K: How about Melville, Hawthorne—American writers of the past? Do you like Twain, for instance?

H: Yes, I know only *Huckleberry Finn*, I guess, and I admire it very much. Melville is the writer I would identify with in the past.

K: Any particular book?

H: *Moby Dick, Billy Budd,* "Bartleby, the Scrivener."

K: Along with comedy, you've called language "a saving grace." Why?

H: It's the best way to make intangibility concrete. It's what's most characteristic of the human being. It's the highest form of paradox—and I like paradox.

K: Your narrators are articulate people.

H: Yes. For me, everything depends on language. The beauty of language is that in its very utterance it is nothing but intelligence being turned into sound, so that in one sense it doesn't exist at all. In another sense, it's the most powerful kind of actuality, so that the paradox of a man behaving through language means that the behavior both exists and does not exist. We can do things with language that we can never do with other forms of action.

K: Is your dislike of Sidney Slyter reflected in his language?

H: His language is pretty good. After all, it's a version of mine.

K: Slyter's glibness, I mean.

н: He's parodying my own language, I guess, as well as journalism, and he's endowed with a poetic voice. He has it both ways. But yes, some of his language reveals his despicableness.

к: Would that be generally true of your fiction? Take Zizendorf, for example.

н: *The Cannibal* was written in the third person and then, in revision, changed to the first person. But the change was merely mechanical, so that the language remains the author's—mine.

к: Do you use language as a structural device?

н: My fiction is largely poetic; its structure generally comes from language itself. Words, images, symbols are thematic carriers loaded with psychic energy.

к: Are you conscious of these?

н: No.

к: Birds appear in your work repeatedly. Are you surprised when somebody brings a thing like that up?

н: I'm no longer very surprised by whatever anybody brings up. A good while ago it became obvious to me the bird imagery had something to do with my own name, but I don't consciously try to insert symbolic materials into my fiction. They're produced in the act of writing and are authentic as such.

к: Have any habits as a writer developed over the years—for instance, kinds of places, time of day, modes of rewriting, quirks, or superstitions?

н: I don't think I have any superstitions about writing. I try to be as unself-conscious about the matter of writing as possible. I like to talk about it, for instance. I don't feel endangered by trying to talk about some projected fiction. I wouldn't hesitate to talk about a novel when it's in progress or give readings from it. I think that the matter of writing is to be as exposed as fully as possible. When I began to write

and finally came to the realization that what I was writing
would be published and that I was in some sense a writer, I
was constantly trying not to live the role of the writer, not to
see writing as anything very special or different from anything else I was doing. I began to write fiction when I was
still in college and wrote *The Cannibal* in Albert Guerard's
writing class at Harvard. I wrote at any time of day or night
and often my wife and various friends were in the room. I
had considerable energy and confidence when I was writing
that first novel and I was quite unaware of the process or its
dangers. I wrote a short novel called *The Owl* in six months
early in the morning from perhaps 6:00 to 8:00 A.M. when
our first child was born and I was working at the Harvard
University Press. Since college I have tended to write in the
morning, for four or five hours at most. Nowadays I find
that I'm only writing two or three hours, but the morning is
still the best time to write, when you are fresh. You ask
where I like to write. I like to write in beautiful, unexpected,
totally new landscapes.

  K: Like Grenada?

  H: Like Grenada. I've written in the West Indies, in
France, and in Greece.

  K: Why is that?

  H: Why the effort to be in a new world?

  K: Yes, almost always a more or less exotic or special
world.

  H: It compensates for the expenditure of energy.
There's a kind of renewal in a fresh landscape, a constant
stimulation of the self and the perceptions, but also being in
a new, unknown place is liberating. It allows me to focus
more clearly on what I'm trying to do. The new landscape is
analogous to the newness of what I'm trying to create. It's a
way of achieving detachment. To be in a new world, a
different world, an unfamiliar world makes the achieve-
ment of detachment easier.

K: You've said that your impulses are largely unconscious and that you get your vision down rather rapidly and
then go back and rework it with great care.

H: I don't think the rapidity is so true, and it would be a
mistake to give the impression that I'm an unconscious
writer. I simply meant that the sources of my fiction come
from deep within the unconscious and that the structure of
what I write is often a matter of images and symbols that
create a pattern because of unconscious consistency, a kind
of consistency in psychic need. *The Beetle Leg* and *The Lime
Twig* are the novels that I rewrote considerably, using charts
and diagrams and painstakingly cutting apart the manus-
cripts and literally saving fragments of sentences and so on.
The first draft of *The Lime Twig* was written in one summer
and revised over a four-year period, off and on. *The Beetle
Leg* was written in about a year and a half and then revised.
So neither one of those short novels was really written that
quickly but both did undergo very elaborate, painstaking
revision. *Second Skin* was written in eight or nine months
and was cut considerably, but not revised too much. *The
Cannibal* was written in about nine months and was hardly
revised at all. It was rearranged at Guerard's suggestion: I
took all the 1914 sections and put them in the middle.
Revision for me, at its best or worst, does mean word by
word, sentence by sentence rewriting, as well as a reasonable amount of reconceiving.

K: So when you talk about revising your materials after
your original conception, you don't mean you consciously
create patterns of imagery?

H: Only in a very minor way. In *Second Skin* I got the
title last, so after I decided on the title I went back and
inserted the phrase once in awhile. For instance, I had
Skipper speak of his "second skin" while putting on the
oilskins. In *The Lime Twig* the title also came last, so after I
had it, when Michael is nauseous in the cab of the truck, I

inserted the word "lime." But the poetic density of the
fiction depends essentially on the initial writing.

ᴋ: You have been labeled existentialist as well as
picaresque. What's your reaction?

ʜ: When I first read Camus's *The Stranger,* I responded
with enormous pleasure to his detachment. I've read a little
bit of Sartre on existentialism only very recently. I'm not
much interested in philosophy, so I don't know much about
existentialism. I suspect it's a pretty humorless matter. On
the other hand, the notion that we are each of us totally
responsible for everything that is, is very much at the center
of what I myself believe. I guess some people have tried to
view my writing as existential because of its insistence on
concrete, physical reality.

ᴋ: And on an absurd world?

ʜ: Yes, cosmic absurdity—the absurdity of life that
does not have any overall cosmic controlling, creating
force—lies at the center of what I write.

ᴋ: Others have lumped you with the surrealists.

ʜ: I appreciate being identified with the surrealists, but
at the same time resist that identification because I don't
think it's very applicable. There's nothing merely murky or
dreamlike about my fiction, and it's not a matter of unconscious flow or automatic writing. I'm interested in highly
shaped and perfected works of art in which the language
and everything in the fiction have to achieve a certain intensity and rightness. The prose in *Charivari* is highly poetic
and that short novel is, I guess, the closest to surrealistic
writing that I've done. *Charivari* probably contains more
unrevised unconscious content than anything else I've written.

ᴋ: Supposedly at a party years ago you said that in
surrealistic works the reader is never informed whether or
not he has entered a dream, but that in your own fiction one
always knows.

H: There are very few literal dreams in my fiction.

K: Aren't there some in *Charivari*?

H: Dreamlike moments, perhaps, but no dreams—that I can recall.

K: Hallucinations?

H: The moments you're thinking of are simply mythical actualities. The difference has to do with the degree of coldness and detachment and ruthlessness in controlling and shaping the material. Paradoxically, soon after I began to write, I knew that I wanted to keep the reader out of the fictional experience, wanted to resist the reader so that he would participate more fully. Surrealism, to me, suggests a kind of indulgence or letting go, the creation of an amorphous world. My fictions at best are hardly amorphous. They are highly textured, but the images and violence are crisply created, sharply done.

K: And yet wouldn't it be fair to say that there is a dreamlike quality, for example, when Michael Banks goes to the widow's parlor? Could the element of distortion here be explained through intoxication?

K: Michael's visit to the widow's parlor is not intended to be a realistic representation of the character's distorted perception. Those scenes that suggest a kind of terrifying familiarity and unfamiliarity, a kind of controlled chaos, come closest, for me, to the true nature of "reality." I'm not interested in portraying the psychic states of characters.

K: This is your world and the characters merely function in it?

H: Yes. I write my own authorial visions of what I take to be "reality."

K: Is the term "anti-realist" appropriate?

H: Sure. That's Albert Guerard's term, though I think he sometimes attributes it to me. It was a term that he substituted for surrealism.

K: What does it mean?

н: I think that what Guerard would probably say is that documentary realism is dead. I'm concerned with the creation of new forms of fiction. If you view these forms in the light of tradition, I suppose you could say that they destroy many expectations that earlier forms created in readers. My real interest in writing is simply to create what didn't exist before.

к: You have said that plot, character, setting, and theme are the worst enemies of the novel. Do you still subscribe to that?

н: Yes. But I myself believe that no form, no kind of fiction has been exhausted. There are certain novels which, I suppose, couldn't be repeated. If somebody now tried to write what appeared to be a Marquand novel we wouldn't be able to read it, but that's not to say that new forms of familiar fiction can't be written and mightn't be quite pure and exciting and extraordinary. I have no set feelings about the limitations of fiction, although I can't read fiction that's written in unenergized language or that seems predictable in its shape. I suspect that conventional novelistic shapes encourage the use of easy, banal language. But I detest worn-out critical terms. They don't have much to do with how I think about the novel. It's with great reluctance that I have to admit even that I create characters. I think of the writing of fiction as the creation of vision, and *The Blood Oranges* is really quite a visionary fiction and only resembles a novel. That it involves a "story" and four characters involved in love affairs is incidental to its treatment of imagination.

к: When you think of a term like realism . . . .

н: It means pedestrian thinking.

к: And pedestrian techniques?

н: Yes.

к: Is it that a world has disappeared and therefore reality cannot be treated in the same old ways?

H: I suppose innumerable worlds have disappeared. And given the loss or diminishing value of so much we accepted—gods, family, afterlife, etc.—and given all we know about our terrifying, destructive possibilities and the courage needed to affirm human potential, any kind of art or fiction that reflects the worn-out, dead, banal views is intolerable.

# Notes

1. John Hawkes, "The Landscape of the Imagination," unpublished transcript of a B.B.C. telediphone recording. November 2, 1966, p. 3.

2. *Ibid.*, pp. 2–3.

3. *Ibid.*, pp. 3–4.

4. John Hawkes, "Flannery O'Connor's Devil," *The Sewanee Review*, LXX (Summer 1962), 399.

5. [John Enck], "John Hawkes: An Interview," *Wisconsin Studies in Comparative Literature*, VI, 2 (Summer 1964), 148.

6. Ernest Jones, *On the Nightmare* (New York: Liveright, 1971), pp. 74–75, 238–39, 44.

7. Jean-Paul Sartre, *Nausea* (New York: New Directions, 1964), pp. 208–9.

8. [Enck], "John Hawkes: An Interview," *Wisconsin Studies in Comparative Literature*, VI, 2 (Summer 1964), 146.

9. *Ibid.*, p. 154.

10. In his introduction to *The Lime Twig* (Norfolk, Connecticut: New Directions, 1961), Leslie A. Fiedler suggested connections between Hawkes's novel and Graham Greene's *Brighton Rock*. Other critics have elaborated on the partallels between the

two books, but the fullest discussion occurs on pp. 101–4 of Frederick Busch's *Hawkes: A Guide to His Fictions* (Syracuse: Syracuse University Press, 1973). Here Busch develops similarities of form, setting, events, characters, and details.

11. John Graham, "John Hawkes on His Novels," *The Massachusetts Review*, VII, 3 (Summer 1966), 455.

12. Robert Graves, *The Greek Myths* (Baltimore: Penguin Books, 1955), Vol. II, p. 358.

13. Tony Tanner, "Necessary Landscapes and Luminous Deteriorations," *TriQuarterly Review*, No. 20 (Winter 1971), 176.

14. Frank Kermode, Introduction to the Arden edition of *The Tempest* (Cambridge, Massachusetts: Harvard University Press, 1958), pp. xlvii–xlviii.

15. Mircea Eliade, *Myth and Reality* (New York: Harper & Row, 1968), pp. 63, 54–55.

16. Sir James George Frazer, *The Golden Bough: A Study in Magic and Religion,* abr. ed. in 1 vol. (New York: The Macmillan Co., 1958), pp. 420–27.

17. *Ibid.*, pp. 434, 439, 442.

18. Jessie L. Weston, *From Ritual to Romance* (Garden City: Doubleday & Co., 1957), pp. 20–21, 125, 55.

19. Graham, "John Hawkes on His Novels," *The Massachusetts Review*, VII, 3 (Summer 1966), 451.

20. *Ibid.*, p. 454.

21. Frazer, *The Golden Bough: A Study in Magic and Religion,* abr. ed. in 1 vol. (New York: The Macmillan Co., 1958), pp. 735, 734.

22. Sigmund Freud, *Civilization and Its Discontents* (Garden City: Doubleday & Co.), pp. 74–75.

23. Graham, "John Hawkes on His Novels," *The Massachusetts Review*, VII, 3 (Summer 1966), p. 450.

24. John Hawkes, "The Voice of Edwin Honig," *Voices*, No. 174 (January–April 1961), 39–47.

25. In a letter to John Kuehl dated September 22, 1965, Hawkes called his story "The Nearest Cemetery" (*The San Francisco Review*, Fall 1963, 374–81) "the preliminary vision out of

which my last novel *Second Skin* was generated." He said that without this "compression of 20–30 handwritten pages" prepared during the summer of 1960 and "the intervening two years of thought" the novel could not have been composed. "The Nearest Cemetery [*sic*] really is a microcosmic version of a good portion of the book," explained Hawkes, who felt there was "much to say about the various transformation" between it and *Second Skin*. These included "the metamorphosis of the island barber as first-person narrator into Skipper as narrator, the transformations of various characters, the expansion of certain metaphors, ideas, etc. what has been retained and what omitted, the transformation of the plot itself." See John Kuehl, ed., *Write and Rewrite: A Study of the Creative Process* (New York: Meredith Press, 1967), pp. 264–87.

26. Sharon Spencer, *Space, Time and Structure in the Modern Novel* (New York: New York University Press, 1971), pp. 155–57.

27. Herbert Blau, Preface to *The Innocent Party* (New York: New Directions, 1966), pp. 9–10.

28. [Enck], "John Hawkes: An Interview," *Wisconsin Studies in Comparative Literature*, VI, 2 (Summer 1964), 149.

29. William Flint Thrall, Addison Hibbard, and C. Hugh Holman, *A Handbook to Literature* (New York: The Odyssey Press, 1960), p. 356.

30. [Enck], "John Hawkes: An Interview," *Wisconsin Studies in Comparative Literature*, VI, 2 (Summer 1964), 151.

31. Hawkes, "The Landscape of the Imagination," unpublished transcript of a B.B.C. telediphone recording, November 2, 1966, pp. 3–4.

32. Robert Scholes, *The Fabulators* (New York: Oxford University Press, 1967), p. 88.

33. [Enck], "John Hawkes: An Interview," *Wisconsin Studies in Comparative Literature*, VI, 2 (Summer 1964), 154–55.

34. Graham, "John Hawkes on His Novels," *The Massachusetts Review*, VII, 3 (Summer 1966), 459.

35. [Enck], "John Hawkes: An Interview," *Wisconsin Studies in Comparative Literature*, VI, 2 (Summer 1964), 155.

36. Hawkes, "The Landscape of the Imagination," unpublished transcript of a B.B.C. telediphone recording, November 2, 1966, p. 6.

37. Graham, "John Hawkes on His Novels," *The Massachusetts Review*, VII, 3 (Summer 1966), 456.

38. [Enck], "John Hawkes: An Interview," *Wisconsin Studies in Comparative Literature*, VI, 2 (Summer 1964), 151.

39. Hawkes, "Flannery O'Connor's Devil," *The Sewanee Review*, LXX (Summer 1962), 397.

40. John Hawkes, "Notes on the Wild Goose Chase," *The Massachusetts Review*, III (Summer 1962), 786–88.

41. Hawkes, "Flannery O'Connor's Devil," *The Sewanee Review*, LXX (Summer 1962), 397.

42. See, for example, pp. 65–69 of the 1965 New Directions edition.

43. Hawkes, "The Landscape of the Imagination," unpublished transcript of a B.B.C. telediphone recording, November 2, 1966, p. 1.

44. [Enck], "John Hawkes: An Interview," *Wisconsin Studies in Comparative Literature*, VI, 2 (Summer 1964), 146.

45. *Ibid.*, p. 149.

46. Richard Chase, *The American Novel and Its Tradition* (Garden City: Doubleday and Co., 1957), pp. 12–13.

47. Frederick Busch, "A John Hawkes Bestiary: Animal Imagery in the Novels of John Hawkes," unpublished master's essay, Columbia University, June, 1967, pp. 4–5, 91, 102, 156.

48. *Ibid.*, pp. 109, 163.

49. Thrall, Hibbard, and Holman, *A Handbook to Literature* (New York: The Odyssey Press, 1960), p. 105.

50. Scholes, *The Fabulators* (New York: Oxford University Press, 1967), p. 99.

51. Graham, "John Hawkes on His Novels," *The Massachusetts Review*, VII, 3 (Summer 1966), 456–57.

52. [Enck], "John Hawkes: An Interview," *Wisconsin Studies in Comparative Literature*, VI, 2 (Summer 1964), 149–50. Hawkes's growing preference for first-person narration may also be seen in

his editorial contribution to *The Personal Voice* (Philadelphia & New York: J. B. Lippincott Co., 1964) and in his participation in the Voice Project at Stanford University (see John Hawkes, "The Voice Project: An Idea for Innovation in the Teaching of Writing," *Writers as Teachers/Teachers as Writers*, ed. Jonathan Baumbach [New York, Chicago, San Francisco: Holt, Rinehart and Winston, 1970], pp. 89–144).

53. *Ibid.*, pp. 150–52.

54. *Ibid.*, p. 150.

55. Hawkes, "Flannery O'Connor's Devil," *The Sewanee Review*, LXX (Summer 1962), 398, 396, 403.

56. Wolfgang Kayser, *The Grotesque in Art and Literature* (New York and Toronto: McGraw-Hill Book Co., 1966), p. 188. The subsequent quotations have been taken from pp. 61, 63–64.

57. [Enck], "John Hawkes: An Interview," *Wisconsin Studies in Comparative Literature*, VI, 2 (Summer 1964), 150.

58. *Ibid.*, p. 155.

59. Earl Rovit, "The Fiction of John Hawkes: An Introductory View," *Modern Fiction Studies*, XI, 2 (Summer 1964), 160.

60. Graham, "John Hawkes on His Novels," *The Massachusetts Review*, VII, 3 (Summer 1966), 459–60.

61. John Graham, comp., *The Merrill Studies in Second Skin* (Columbus, Ohio: Charles E. Merrill Publishing Co., 1971).

62. Thrall, Hibbard, and Holman, *A Handbook to Literature* (New York: The Odyssey Press, 1960), p. 242.

63. Unpublished letters from John Hawkes to John Kuehl of November 10, 1972, April 19, 1973, February 10, 1972, and February 22, 1972, respectively.

64. Robert Scholes, "A Conversation on *The Blood Oranges* Between John Hawkes and Robert Scholes," *Novel*, V, 3 (Spring 1972), 203.

65. *Ibid.*, pp. 202, 207.

66. J. E. Circlot, *A Dictionary of Symbols* (New York: Philosophical Library, 1962), p. 50.

67. Scholes, "A Conversation on *The Blood Oranges* Between John Hawkes and Robert Scholes," *Novel*, V, 3 (Spring 1972), 200.

68. Thrall, Hibbard, and Holman, *A Handbook to Literature* (New York: The Odyssey Press, 1960), p. 230.

69. Scholes, "A Conversation on *The Blood Oranges* Between John Hawkes and Robert Scholes," *Novel*, V, 3 (Spring 1972), 200.

70. Aaron Copland, *What to Listen for in Music* (New York: The New American Library, 1953), p. 58.

71. C. L. Barnhart and Jess Stein (eds.), *The American College Dictionary* (New York: Random House, 1963), p. 887.

72. Scholes, "A Conversation on *The Blood Oranges* Between John Hawkes and Robert Scholes," *Novel*, V, 3 (Spring 1972), 198.

73. *Ibid.*, p. 200.

74. All *The Good Soldier* quotations have been taken from the Vintage Book edition (New York: Random House, Inc., 1955).

75. Scholes, "A Conversation on *The Blood Oranges* Between John Hawkes and Robert Scholes," *Novel*, V, 3 (Spring 1972), 199–200.

# Bibliography

This bibliography is selective. It should be supplemented by other bibliographies: Jackson R. Bryer's in *Critique*, VI, 2 (Fall 1963), 89–94; Frederick Busch's in *Hawkes: A Guide to His Fictions*, Syracuse University Press, 1973; Donald Greiner's in *Comic Terror*, Memphis State University Press, 1974; and Marshall C. Old's unpublished bibliography.

## WRITINGS BY HAWKES

### POETRY

*Fiasco Hall*. Cambridge, Massachusetts: Harvard University Printing Office, 1943.

"Little Beatrice," *Harvard Advocate*, CXXX (April 28, 1947), 12.

"The Magic House of Christopher Smart," *Harvard Advocate*, CXXX (May 21, 1947), 14.

### PLAYS

*The Innocent Party: Four Short Plays by John Hawkes*. New York: New Directions, 1966. Includes: *The Innocent Party*, *The Wax Museum*, *The Undertaker*, *The Questions*.

STORIES AND SHORT NOVELS

*Lunar Landscapes: Stories & Short Novels 1950–1963.* New York: New Directions, 1969. Includes: "The Traveler" (1962), "The Grandmother" (1961), "A Little Bit of the Old Slap and Tickle" (1962), "Death of an Airman" (1950), "A Song Outside" (1962), "The Nearest Cemetery" (1963), *Charivari* (1950), *The Owl* (1954), *The Goose on the Grave* (1954).

"The Universal Fears," *American Review 16* (February 1973), 108–23.

NOVELS

*The Cannibal.* Norfolk, Connecticut: New Directions, 1949.
*The Beetle Leg.* New York: New Directions, 1951.
*The Lime Twig.* Norfolk, Connecticut: New Directions, 1961.
*Second Skin.* New York: New Directions, 1964.
*The Blood Oranges.* New York: New Directions, 1971.
*Death, Sleep & the Traveler.* New York: New Directions, 1974.

INTERVIEWS

With John Enck. "John Hawkes: An Interview." *Wisconsin Studies in Comparative Literature*, VI, 2 (Summer 1964), 141–55.

With John Graham. "John Hawkes on His Novels." *The Massachusetts Review*, VII, 3 (Summer 1966), 449–61.

With David Keyser and Ned French. "Talks with John Hawkes." *Harvard Advocate*, CIV, 2 (October 1970), 6, 34–35.

With Robert Scholes. "A Conversation on *The Blood Oranges* Between John Hawkes and Robert Scholes," *Novel*, V, 3 (Spring 1972), 197–207.

CRITICISM AND OTHER NON-FICTION

"Notes on Violence." *Audience*, VII (Spring 1960), 60.

"The Voice of Edwin Honig." *Voices*, No. 174 (January–April 1961), 39–47.

"Flannery O'Connor's Devil." *The Sewanee Review*, LXX (Summer 1962), 395–407.

"Notes on the Wild Goose Chase." *The Massachusetts Review*, III (Summer 1962), 784–88.

Ed. with Guerard, Albert J.; Guerard, Maclin B.; and Rosenfield, Claire. *The Personal Voice: A Contemporary Prose Reader*. Philadelphia and New York: J. B. Lippincott Co., 1964.

"The Landscape of the Imagination," transcript of a telediphone recording of BBC broadcast, November 2, 1966. (Part of a symposium with George Macbeth and others.)

"The Voice Project: An Idea for Innovation in the Teaching of Writing." In *Writers as Teachers/Teachers as Writers*, edited by Jonathan Baumbach. New York, Chicago, and San Francisco: Holt, Rinehart and Winston, 1970.


WRITINGS ABOUT HAWKES

Busch, Frederick. *Hawkes: A Guide to His Fictions*. Syracuse: Syracuse University Press, 1973.

————. "A John Hawkes Bestiary: Animal Imagery in the Novels of John Hawkes." Unpublished master's essay. Columbia University, June, 1967.

*Critique*, VI, 2 (Fall 1963). John Hawkes and John Barth Issue. Includes, besides Jackson R. Bryer's bibliography, articles by: Alan Trachtenberg, "Barth and Hawkes: Two Fabulists"; Albert J. Guerard, "The Prose Style of John Hawkes"; D. P. Reutlinger, "*The Cannibal:* 'The Reality of Victim' "; Charles Matthews, "The Destructive Vision of John Hawkes."

Edenbaum, Robert I. "John Hawkes: *The Lime Twig* and Other Tenuous Horrors." *The Massachusetts Review*, VII, 3 (Summer 1966), 462–75.

Fiedler, Leslie A. "A Lonely American Eccentric: The Pleasures of John Hawkes." *The New Leader*, XLIII (December 12, 1960), 12–14.

Frost, Lucy. "The Crowning of American Adam: Hawkes' *The Beetle Leg*." *Critique*, XIV (Summer 1973), 63–74.

Graham, John, comp. *The Merrill Studies in Second Skin*. Columbus, Ohio: Charles E. Merrill Publishing Company, 1971. Includes: "Contemporary Reviews," "Observations by

Hawkes," "The Growth of *Second Skin*," and "Essays." The "Essays" include: S. K. Oberbeck, "John Hawkes: The Smile Slashed by a Razor"; Lucy Frost, "Awakening Paradise"; William R. Robinson, "John Hawkes' Artificial Inseminator"; Stephen G. Nichols, Jr., "Vision and Tradition in *Second Skin*"; Anthony C. Santore, "Narrative Unreliability and the Structure of *Second Skin*"; Albert J. Guerard, *"Second Skin: The Light and Dark Affirmation."*

Green, James L. "Nightmare and Fairy Tale in Hawkes' 'Charivari.' " *Critique*, XIII, 1 (1971), 83–95.

Greiner, Donald. "The Thematic Use of Color in John Hawkes's *Second Skin*." *Contemporary Literature*, XI, 3 (Summer 1970), 389–400.

———. "Strange Laughter: The Comedy of John Hawkes." *Southwest Review*, LVI (Autumn 1971), 318–28.

———. *Comic Terror*. Memphis: Memphis State University Press, 1974.

Guerard, Albert J. "Introduction to the Cambridge Anti-Realists." *Audience*, VII (Spring 1960), 57–59.

———. "Addendum" and "Introduction" in *The Cannibal*.

Norfolk, Connecticut: New Directions Paperbook, 1962, pp. ix–xx.

———. "John Hawkes in English J." *Harvard Advocate*, CIV, 2 (October 1970), 10.

———. "Illuminating Distortion." *Novel*, V (Winter 1972), 101–21.

Kuehl, John, ed. *Write and Rewrite: A Study of the Creative Process*. New York: Meredith Press, 1967. Chapter 9, "Story Into Novel," includes a headnote and commentary by Kuehl, "The Nearest Cemetery," and two excerpts from *Second Skin*.

Lavers, Norman. "The Structure of *Second Skin*." *Novel*, V, 3 (Spring 1972), 208–14.

Malin, Irving. *New American Gothic*. Carbondale: Southern Illinois University Press, 1962. See pp. 38–44, 71–75, 99–103, 124–26, 159–60.

Moran, Charles. "John Hawkes: Paradise Gaining." *The Massachusetts Review*, XII, 4 (Autumn 1971), 840–45.

Pearce, Richard. *Stages of the Clown*. Carbondale: Southern Illinois University Press, 1970. See pp. 102–16, "Harlequin: The Character of the Clown in Saul Bellow's *Henderson the Rain King* and John Hawkes's *Second Skin*."

Ratner, Marc. "The Constructed Vision: The Fiction of John Hawkes." *Studi Americani* (Roma), XI (1965), 345–57.

Romano, John. "Our Best-Known Neglected Novelist." *Commentary*, LVII, 5 (May 1974), 58–60.

Rosenfield, Claire. "John Hawkes: Nightmares of the Real." *The Minnesota Review*, II (Winter 1962), 249–54.

Rovit, Earl. "The Fiction of John Hawkes: An Introductory View." *Modern Fiction Studies*, XI, 2 (Summer 1964), 150–62.

Scholes, Robert. *The Fabulators*. New York: Oxford University Press, 1967. Chapter 4, "Fabulation and Picaresque," includes "Black Humor in Hawkes and Southern," "John Hawkes's Theory of Fiction," and "*The Lime Twig*."

Schott, Webster. "Vision of Nightmare." *The Nation*, CXCIII (September 2, 1961), 122–23.

———. "John Hawkes, American Original." *New York Times Book Review*, May 29, 1966, pp. 4, 24–25.

Shepherd, Allen. "Illumination Through (Anti) Climax: John Hawkes' *The Lime Twig*." *Notes on Contemporary Literature*, II, 2 (March 1972), 11–13.

Stubbs, John. "John Hawkes and the Dream-Work of *The Lime Twig* and *Second Skin*." *Literature and Psychology*, XXI, 3 (1971), 149–60.

Tanner, Tony. "Necessary Landscapes and Luminous Deteriorations." *TriQuarterly Review*, No. 20 (Winter 1971), 145–79. See also *City of Words* (New York: Harper, 1971), pp. 202–29.